Abide in Me

Abide in Me

A STUDY OF THE
COVENANTAL TRINITY

RALPH ALLAN SMITH

Abide in Me: A Study of the Covenantal Trinity
By Ralph Allan Smith

Copyright © 2026 Ralph Allan Smith

Athanasius Press
715 Cypress Street
West Monroe, Louisiana, 71291
www.athanasiuspress.org

Cover design and typesetting: Rachel Rosales

ISBN: 978-1-957726-21-2

Unless specified otherwise, all Scripture quotations are taken from the New King James Version®. Copyright © 1982 by Thomas Nelson. Used by permission. All rights reserved.

Printed in the United States of America.

CONTENTS

This book is dedicated to J. Steven Wilkins,
pastor of the Church of the Redeemer in West Monroe,
Louisiana because of my respect for his faithful pastoral
labors for many years, his courage in standing for the
Gospel in the face of opposition, and my appreciation
for his personal kindness to me.

Blessed are the peacemakers,
For they shall be called sons of God.
Blessed are those who are persecuted for righteousness' sake,
For theirs is the kingdom of heaven.
Matthew 5:9-10

PREFACE

This short book is a meditation on a subject that has occupied me for many years. Sometime in the late 1980s, I was introduced to this topic by James Jordan. Since then, through their various writings, he and Peter Leithart have guided and stimulated my thinking. Of course, as the footnotes indicate, there have been others. I personally regard the archetypal covenant among the Persons of the Trinity as the most fundamental and important insight on the subject of the covenant in the Bible and a profound contribution to biblical thinking about the Triune God, our Savior and Lord. I hope this book might be used to introduce others to this topic and encourage deeper work in the future.

INTRODUCTION

This book argues that the biblical doctrine of the covenant has its roots in the biblical teaching about the Triune God. This is an unusual view—in spite of the fact that most biblical scholars, and not just Reformed scholars, recognize the centrality or at least the tremendous importance of the covenant idea in the Bible. Dispensationalists, for all their opposition to covenant theology, still have a place in their system for God's covenants with Abraham, Moses, and David, and, of course, for the New Covenant as well.[1] Walter Kaiser's suggestion that the "promise-plan" of God supplies an exegetical meta-narrative still relies heavily on the covenants with Abraham and David.[2] John H. Walton believes that his approach to biblical covenants incorporates the best insights of dispensationalists and covenant theologians to give the biblical doctrine

---

[1] See Charles Ryrie, *The Basis of the Premillennial Faith* (Neptune, NJ: Loizeaux Brothers, 1953), 48-125, an extended exposition of the dispensational view of the Abrahamic, Davidic, and New covenants. See also, *Dispensationalism* (Chicago: Moody Press, 1995), 135ff.

[2] Walter Kaiser, *The Promise Plan of God* (Grand Rapids: Zondervan, 2008). In criticizing what he calls the "super covenant"—his name for reformed theology—Kaiser speaks of "the covenants that are used by the Scriptures to organize the unity of the Bible."

of the covenant its proper place.[3] N. T. Wright, whose theology can be called "Reformed," also emphasizes the covenant theme of Scripture,[4] even though he certainly does not employ the Westminster idea of a Covenant of Works and a Covenant of Grace. In short, to borrow from Gentry and Wellum, "In fact, almost every variety of Christian theology admits that the biblical covenants establish a central framework that holds the story of the Bible together."[5]

It had to be so, for the word "covenant" appears so often in Scripture and in places so prominent for the whole flow of the biblical story that no one who takes Scripture seriously can ignore it. But Reformed theology—since it is historically "covenant theology" and attempts to offer a definitive approach to the biblical idea of "covenant"— ironically faces special problems. For one thing, Presbyterian theologians have been unable to agree on a definition of the biblical idea of "covenant."[6] The Westminster Stan-

---

[3] John H. Walton, *Covenant: God's Purpose, God's Plan* (Grand Rapids: Zondervan, 1994).

[4] For example: N. T. Wright, *The Climax of the Covenant: Christ and the Law in Pauline Theology* (Minneapolis: Fortress Press, 1992).

[5] Peter J. Gentry, Stephen J. Wellum. "Kingdom through Covenant." Apple Books. See also Daniel Block's massive work, *Covenant: The Framework of God's Grand Plan of Redemption* (Grand Rapids: Baker Academic, 2021). Though Block, like Gentry and Wellum, rightly sees the covenant as the "framework" for God's plan, he defines covenant as an agreement, or pact, missing the heart of the covenant idea.

[6] See William B. Evans for a whole host of problems with Reformed views of the covenant. "Deja Vu All Over Again? The Contemporary Reformed Soteriological Controversy In Historical Perspective," in

dards actually gave them a bad start. Presbyterians who believe the Bible and take their standards seriously are yoked with a bi-covenantal system that finds little or no support from biblical exegesis. Worse, a serious study of Genesis 1-2 precludes the very possibility of a Covenant of Works—the weak link in the bi-covenantal system—because God's relationship with man from the beginning, though covenantal for sure, was wholly and abundantly gracious.[7] Contrary to what the works paradigm would suggest—if its logic were followed—Adam was not promised that obedience to God's command during a period of trial would give him an entrance into the Garden-sanctu-

---

Westminster Theological Journal, 72:1 (Spring, 2010), 135ff. Evans wrote: "But the history of the tradition shows that Reformed theologians have been arguing over issues of covenant definition, as well as the dialectic of covenant conditionality and unconditionality for almost four hundred years, and these debates are not abating" (149).

[7] In expounding the "Covenant of Works," Reformed theologians characteristically emphasize the gracious nature of the relationship established. Adam's probation was limited in time, but the reward was eternal. The work required of Adam was simply not to eat from the Tree of the Knowledge of Good and Evil, a very simple task. If Adam had obeyed, not only Adam, but also all his descendants would have been rewarded with eternal life. These and other aspects of the arrangement are cited to show that the Covenant of Works is full of grace and to demonstrate the goodness of God in granting it. But even when the grace of the arrangement is emphasized, Adam is still placed upon probation and must earn his justification by works. Thus, our justification also is understood in this framework. Jesus had to keep the Covenant of Works and earn justification for all who believe in Him, for all the elect. See, for example, "Lecture XII. The Covenant of Works," in *The Collected Writings of James Henley Thornwell, Volume 1. Theological* (Edinburgh: Banner of Truth Trust, 1974), 254-300.

ary to have fellowship with God. On the contrary, he was placed in the Garden-sanctuary by grace from the beginning. In this and many other particulars, the Westminster paradigm forced Presbyterian theologians to fit biblical revelation into a procrustean bi-covenantal bed, which, historically cut off potential for theological growth and development.[8]

Dutch Reformed theology, though originally holding to the same bi-covenantal arrangement,[9] was not bound by confessional standards to press everything covenantal into that mold. With Abraham Kuyper especially, it developed covenantal theology in fruitful ways that stand behind this present work.

But there is a more recent Reformed approach to the biblical idea of covenant, one that is worse by far than the Westminster misconception. I am referring to John Stek's view, endorsed by William B. Evans, that Reformed theology suffers from "covenant overload."[10] Why overload? Because, as Evans explains, 1) "the cove-

---

[8] I hasten to add that one can be a faithful Westminster Presbyterian without following the traditional Covenant of Works in his theology and most, though not all, Presbyterian theologians who do hold the Covenant of Works emphasize the gracious character of the Covenant of Works.

[9] Geerhardus Vos, to take just one example, though in the Dutch Reformed tradition, held to a covenant of works/covenant of grace system. See the many references in Vos, *Reformed Dogmatics, Volume Four: Soteriology, The Application of the Merits of the Mediator by the Holy Spirit* (Bellingham, WA: Lexham Press, 2015).

[10] Evans, Op. cit., 150. Also, https://theecclesialcalvinist.wordpress.com/2013/08/09/lets-rethink-this-covenant-issue-shall-we/

nant theme in Scripture emerges as an accommodation to the ancient Near Eastern cultural context," 2) so that, "it was never intended as a timeless and all-encompassing organizing principle of theology," 3) but that "covenant is a 'secondary biblical theme' that functions within relationships already constituted."[11] Evans is not alone in this. All of the "worlds" that John Walton has lost share the same basic fallacy, as do many other Old Testament theologies and expositions.[12]

What do I mean that this recent idea is worse than Westminster's mistaken bi-covenantal paradigm? First, to say that "the covenant theme in Scripture emerges as an accommodation to the ancient Near Eastern cultural context" is to say that the God who reveals Himself in Holy Scripture seems to have been "forced" to fit into the ancient Near Eastern cultural context to make Himself known. This is blatantly wrong for two very important reasons. One, the Bible is constantly contradicting Israel's cultural context. Why would God have to accommodate Himself in this particular case when He offers the most forceful opposition to this cultural context in so many other instances?

Second, more importantly, the Bible itself puts ancient Near Eastern culture into the context of biblical history and revelation. Note well: in the Bible, the ancient

---

[11] Ibid.

[12] Just to cite the titles of the books of John Walton's lost worlds (with more worlds to be lost in the future, no doubt): *The Lost World Scripture, The Lost World of Genesis One, The Lost World of Adam and Eve, The Lost World of the Flood, The Lost World of Torah, The Lost World of Israelite Conquest.*

Near East is not some neutral culture that evolved from nowhere that God must pander to in order to communicate with Abraham and others. Quite the contrary, as the Bible shows, the ancient Near East is the heir to Noah, largely through his perverse descendant Nimrod, a mighty hunter *against* Yahweh (Gen. 10:9) and the head of the Babel project, a rebellion against God.[13] Nimrod and his cohorts inherited cultural and religious ideas from Noah, but distorted them. All of ancient Near Eastern culture—not to mention that of the rest of humanity, who were also descended from Noah—in one way or another, to one degree or another, inherited the Noahic worldview, distorted through Nimrod and Babel. The biblical God was not forced to accommodate the ancient Near Eastern pagan culture which had perverted His prior revelation to Noah. The ancient Near East's worldviews are malformed accommodations to the Bible's worldview as it was known in the days after Noah. Ancient Israel, therefore, has much in common with the Ancient Near East in general because they are ultimately descended from the same source, but only in the Bible is the source preserved in its purity.

Was "covenant" intended as a "timeless" principle? In one sense, the clear answer to this is obviously, "No," for the Bible itself gives us a series of covenants, each dependent upon and developing previous covenants. But that does not mean that the covenant idea cannot be an "all-encompassing organizing principle of theology."

---

[13] See Peter J. Leithart, *Between Babel and Beast: America and Empires in Biblical Perspective* (Eugene, OR: Cascade Books, 2012), 4-8.

Why not? Consider: if the development of covenants within the historical plan of God reflects and manifests something more fundamental, something prior to creation, then the historical covenants point to something transcendent, something that might be called an "all-encompassing organizing principle of theology."

I will argue that "covenant" is not a "secondary biblical theme," but the most fundamental relationship imaginable. Thomas Torrance used the expression "onto-relational" to describe the relationships among the Persons of the Trinity.[14] I want to add that, in the Bible, God's relationships to the created world are presented as covenantal, that all God's relationships with man are presented as covenantal, and that also relationships among men are inescapably covenantal. I will argue that the reason for this pervasive notion of covenantal relations is that the "onto-relations" among the Trinitarian Persons are more properly understood as "onto-covenantal" relations.[15]

---

[14] Thomas F. Torrance, *The Christian Doctrine of God, One Being-Three Persons* (London: Bloomsbury T&T Clark, 2016). To cite just one example of this idea: "It was in connection with this refined conception of *perichoresis* in its employment to speak of the intra-trinitarian relations in God, that Christian theology developed what I have long called its *onto-relational* concept of the divine Persons, or an understanding of the three divine Persons in the one God in which the ontic relations between them belong to what they essentially are in themselves in their distinctive *hypostases*. Along with this there developed out of the doctrine of the Trinity the new *concept of person,* unknown in human thought until then, according to which the relations between persons belong to what persons are" (102).

[15] See also my essay, "A Covenantal Ontology of the Triune God," https://www.berith.org/pdf/A-Covenantal-Ontology-of-the-Tri-

Obviously, this thesis is not new to me,[16] but it has not often been argued for. I hope to show that the relationships among the Persons of the Trinity are presented in language that the Bible consistently uses of covenants. Following Abraham Kuyper, I will argue that the reason for the pervasiveness of covenantal language and covenantal relationships in the Bible is that God's covenants with creation and with men reflect who He is in Himself.

What difference does that make? The answer to this question is provided, at least partially, by an essay written by Robert Jenson: "What Kind of God Can Make a Covenant?"[17] His answer begins: "Let me suggest that making a covenant would take a very particular, indeed a quite odd kind of God—or at least odd by the standards of the main Western intellectual tradition." The "god" of the ancient Greek thinkers would never speak with men and certainly never negotiate with Abraham over the fate of Sodom! The kind of God who could and would make a covenant must be the Creator, a Creator who cares for His creation and who maintains an intimate relationship to the world He has made—unlike the "god" of deism, for example. As Jenson's outstanding essay proceeds through Scriptural stories and theological interpretations,

---

une-God.pdf

[16] I first learned of this from James B. Jordan, *The Law of the Covenant: An Exposition of Exodus 21-23* (Tyler, Texas: Institute for Christian Economics, 1984).

[17] In *Covenant and Hope: Christian and Jewish Reflections,* edited by Robert W. Jenson and Eugene B. Korn, (Grand Rapids: Eerdmans, 2012) 3–18.

he shows that only the Triune God of Scripture could or would make a covenant.

But Jenson does not take us all the way. Though it is true that only a Triune God who created the world by His Word and Spirit could and would make a covenant, we must go one step further and say that only a Triune God whose very life is a life of covenantal fellowship—a Triune God whose ontology is covenantal—only this sort of God could and would covenant with the world that He created as well as with mankind His image. And because His Triune being is covenantal, all the drama of biblical history, from creation to the New Jerusalem, is inescapably Trinitarian and covenantal. Every Word of Scripture is a Triune Word—the Father speaking the Word by His Spirit. Every relationship with God from creation to consummation is a covenant relationship.

CHAPTER 1

THE FOUNDATION
OF THE COVENANT

The assertion this book makes and expounds is that the Father, Son, and Spirit live a life of covenant love and fellowship that is essential to who they are. But this is not directly taught in the Bible. Rather, in Scripture, what we see is that God makes covenants, gives covenants to Abraham, Moses, and David, for example. In that sense, "covenant" appears to be something God does. Covenant appears to be the way that He relates to creatures. How then or why would one claim that the idea of covenant describes the rich overflowing mutual love and fellowship of Father, Son, and Spirit? What is the basis for such an assertion?

The foundation of the idea that there is a covenant among the Persons of the Triune God is nothing abstract, but, in fact, the very same basis for all that we know about

God. With respect to the Trinity, theologians speak of the "economic Trinity" and the "ontological Trinity." What do these expressions mean? "Economic Trinity" refers to what we know about the Triune God from what He does in history, including His self-revelation in Scripture. "Ontological Trinity" refers to the Triune God as He is in Himself, apart from His relationships with man and other created things.

Why make the distinction? Is it helpful? Yes! It is more than helpful; it is essential. On the one hand, all that we know of God is what He has revealed about Himself. We have no direct insights into His essence and our knowledge of Him, though true and accurate as far as it goes since it depends on His self-revelation, can never be exhaustive. God is absolutely infinite, which means that we can continue to learn and know more of Him for all eternity and still not even begin to fathom the depths of His transcendent beauty and goodness, though nothing new that we will learn will contradict what He has already shown us of Himself.

Through the incarnation and the gift of the Spirit at Pentecost, God has revealed Himself to us as Father, Son, and Spirit. How are we to understand that? How are we to interpret that revelation? Two ancient heresies show us how *not* to interpret God's revelation: "Sabellianism" and "Arianism." "Sabellianism" is named after one of its prominent teachers, Sabellius. This heresy, also called "modalism," a more recent designation, taught that the Father, Son, and Spirit are simply different "modes" of God's existence, not different persons. David Bernard, a leading theologian of the Oneness Pentecostal movement describes it in these words: "In particular, the modalists objected to the concept of a plurality of persons and maintained that Father, Son, and Spirit were three titles of one God."[1] In this view, when the Bible talks of the Father, it is simply describing God doing fatherly things. When it speaks of Him as Son, God is doing filial things. Just like Mr. Jones can be son to his own father, husband to his wife, father to his son, and a teacher or a businessman, every man and woman has several roles in life and different names describe these roles. Sabellianism and Oneness Pentecostalism asserts that God can only be one person.

Arianism, which is much like the theology of the Jehovah's Witnesses, also claims that God Himself can only be one person. For the Arians, the Son is a creature—the first and the greatest creature, but a creature all the same. God is one absolute being who created the Son in time, so they can say that there was a time when the Son did not exist. Like the Sabellians, Arians *know* that God cannot be a Trinity and that biblical revelation suggesting that He is a Trinity must be interpreted according to their presupposition about God being an absolute One. Their objections to trinitarianism are rationalistic, not grounded in revelation. In other words, they claim to know God as He exists in Himself for all eternity even though the God they believe in is very different from the God we see in His revelation.

---

[1] David K. Bernard, *Oneness and Trinity A. D. 100-300: The Doctrine of God in Ancient Christian Writings* (Hazelwood, MO: Word Aflame Press, 1991) 146.

Trinitarianism, on the other hand, insists that God, as He has revealed Himself in His relationship with creation—the economic Trinity—reflects who He is in Himself, apart from His relationship with creation—the ontological Trinity. Biblical Christianity insists that God in Scripture and history reveals Himself to us as He really and eternally is. We see what He has done and hear His word to know God as He is in Himself. This is the foundation of Trinitarian faith—our faith that God is One in essence, but Three in Person—but it is also the foundation for the idea that there is an eternal covenant among the Persons of the Trinity.

How does that work? When we turn to the Scripture to see how God characteristically acts, we note that everywhere and always God relates to creatures in and through covenant. This is clear from the beginning since the process of creation itself was a covenantal process. To understand the importance of this, it is helpful to contrast what I am saying with a common misunderstanding.

It is *not* the case that God created the world first and then later granted a covenant to Adam, as is often presented in Reformed covenant theology. Rowland Ward, for example, suggests that God gave Adam a covenant in Genesis 2:16-17 when He forbade Adam to eat from the Tree of the Knowledge of Good and Evil. Ward quotes Donald Macleod:

> There is nothing inherently improper in a covenant of works. Our very salvation rests on the obedience of the Last Adam and that obedience was compliance with a covenant of works.

Christ saved us by finishing the work given him to do (John 17:4). He was 'obedient unto death' (Phil. 2:8). 'By the obedience of the one shall many be made righteous' (Rom. 5:19). There were indeed gracious elements in the covenant of works. But we must accept that the primary relationship between God and man is a relationship of works and obedience.[2]

But this is not what we actually see in the book of Genesis. James Jordan writes, "The creation narrative describes God's making the world over the course of a week. God's work is cosmic and covenantal. The language in Genesis 1 is used in covenant-making events later on in the Bible . . ."[3] What Jordan is referring to is the strange way God creates: 1) He commands light to be; 2) the not-yet-existing light obeys God's Word and comes into being; 3) God evaluates what He has done; 4) He blesses. Something like this pattern is repeated throughout the creation process and this is what Jordan is calling "covenantal." That means that when God created Adam, He made Adam with covenantal dust and breathed into him covenantal breath. The whole world around Adam was a covenantal world. Not one atom existed apart from God's covenant.

---

[2] Rowland S. Ward, *God and Adam: Reformed Theology and the Creation Covenant* (p. 189). Tulip Publishing. Kindle Edition.

[3] James B. Jordan, *Creation in Six Days: A Defense of the Traditional Reading of Genesis One* (Moscow, ID: Canon Press, 1999), 173.

Thus, Adam was not *given* a covenant; he was created *into* a covenantal relationship. Though Adam never breathed a non-covenantal instant, could not this have still been a covenant of works? Was not Adam's relationship to God primarily one of works and obedience? Not at all. Remember the story. After God created Adam (Gen. 2:7), Adam watched while God made a Garden for His beloved son, and then God placed Adam in the Garden (2:8). Adam's life itself was a gift and blessing and so was the Garden of Eden with all of its trees and fruit. Adam was not required to work or merit his way into the Garden of blessing. Nor was he required to earn his wife—the naming of the animals was "work" in a manner of speaking, but it was part of the heavenly Father teaching His son in preparation for blessing. The whole creation story is about a loving Father graciously bestowing blessing on the son He cherishes. The obedience Adam owed was the obedience of a son responding in love to his Father's love. That is the primary relationship in the Garden and it continued in this way, even, in the law of Moses.[4]

Works and obedience are important, but they are not primary. True faith works, but it works by love (Gal. 5:6). The Father commanded Jesus in love and Jesus responded in love: "I do as the Father has commanded me, so that the world may know that I love the Father" (John 14:31). It is the same in our relationship to God also: "He who has My commandments and keeps them, it is he who

---

[4] See Ralph Allan Smith, *Hear My Son: An Examination of the Fatherhood of Yahweh in Deuteronomy* (Monroe, LA: Athanasius Press, 2011).

loves Me. And he who loves Me will be loved by My Father, and I will love him and manifest Myself to him" (John 14:21).

Thus, though there is no Covenant of Works in the Bible, we do see that from Genesis 1:1 forward, all that God does, He does in in covenant and in a covenantal way. If God's work in history reveals who He is in Himself, we have to ask what does the idea of covenant have to do with God in Himself? Did He become a covenant-making Person in order to relate to creation or does the covenant idea point to something deeper? The biblical answer is that the notion of covenant is not merely how God relates to creatures, for the Bible shows us that the Father and Son also relate in covenant. Reformed theologians point to the fact that the Father covenanted with the Son in what is called the Covenant of Redemption or the *Pactum Salutis*. It is undeniable that the God who said "Let us make man in our image," while planning the creation of mankind, surely planned the incarnation, not to mention all of history, including the fall of a sparrow. Father, Son, and Spirit planned the incarnation and the work of the cross for the salvation of man, as the Gospel of John, repeatedly shows when it speaks of the Son having been "sent." He was clearly sent with a mission. The mission itself could not have been planned at the last minute, so to speak, for Jesus was the lamb slain before the foundation of the world (Rev. 13:8; 17:8). Jesus was obedient to the Father unto death, not because of His own sin or fault, but because He identified Himself with sinful humanity and became the head of a new race, taking on death in order to rise to new life.

Though some Reformed theologians deny there is a Covenant of Redemption, most believe that the plan for the Son to become man and go to the cross suggests a covenantal relationship between the Father and the Son. Assuming that is the case, what does it imply about the Trinity? Here Abraham Kuyper is helpful.

> If the idea of the covenant with regard to man and among men can only occur in its ectypal form, and if its archetypical original is found in the divine economy, then it cannot have its deepest ground in the *pactum salutis* that has its motive in the fall of man. For in that case it would not belong to the divine economy as such, but would be introduced in it rather incidentally and change the essential relations of the Three Persons in the divine Essence. . . . We then confess that in the one personality of the divine Essence there consists a three-personal distinction, which has in the covenant relation its unity and an inseparable tie. God Himself is, according to this conception, not only of every covenant, but of the covenant idea as such the living and eternal foundation; and the essential unity [of the Godhead] has in the covenant relation its conscious expression.[5]

---

[5] Quotation from Herman Hoeksema, *Reformed Dogmatics* (Grand Rapids: Reformed Free Publishing Association, 1985), 295. See also, Ralph A. Smith, *Paradox and Truth: Rethinking Van Til on the Trinity by Comparing Van Til, Plantinga, and Kuyper* (Moscow, ID: Canon Press, 2002). Chapter Four of this book offers evidence from other

Kuyper says, in other words, that God's covenants with men, and even more the covenant between Father and Son, reveal something of the kind of God He is, something deep about His life as a Triune God. God is not only the living and eternal foundation for every covenant that He has made with men, but of the covenant idea itself because the eternal relationships of Father, Son, and Spirit are covenantal.

In line with Kuyper's theology of the covenant, James Jordan offered a definition of the covenant idea from a biblical theology perspective: "*The covenant is a personal-structural bond which joins the three Persons of God in a community of life, and in which man was created to participate.*"[6] That the Persons of the Trinity are united in a community of life, united in the bond of the covenant, is the foundation for the fact that God always relates to the creation and most especially His image, mankind, in covenant. God's covenants with men, therefore, though they are multifaceted, can never be mere agreements or

---

Reformed theologians as well. Kuyper's language "in the one personality of the divine Essence there consists a three-personal distinction" may have been partially the source for Van Til's formula that God is One Person and God is Three Persons. Frame explains, "With regard to the doctrine of the Trinity, Van Til denies that the paradox of the three and one can be resolved by the formula 'one in essence and three in person.' Rather, 'We do assert that God, that is, the whole Godhead, is one person.' Van Til's doctrine, then, can be expressed 'One person, three persons'—an apparent contradiction. This is a very bold theological move." John Frame, *Van Til: The Theologian* (https://frame-poythress.org/van-til-the-theologian/), 14.

[6] James B. Jordan, *The Law of the Covenant: An Exposition of Exodus 21-23* (Tyler, TX: Institute for Christian Economics, 1984), 5.

contracts. A covenant may include statutes and ordinances as loving Paternal instruction, but no covenant given by God to His people can be reduced to "law," for all covenants are graciously given and express the love of Father, Son, and Spirit for the people He saves.

To conclude, then, we know that the Father, Son, and Spirit share a covenantal bond of love and life because everywhere and always the Triune God reveals Himself as a covenantal God, and we know that He is in eternity (the ontological Trinity) as He reveals Himself to us in word and works (the economical Trinity).

CHAPTER 2

THE ESSENCE OF
THE COVENANT

In this chapter, we will consider the question: What is the essence of the covenant among the Persons of the Trinity? The place to begin is by recalling Jordan's definition of the covenant: "*The Covenant is a personal-structural bond which joins the three Persons of God in a community of life, and in which man was created to participate.*"[1] In Jordan's definition, I want to especially consider the word "bond." Jordan says it is a "personal-structural bond," but I want to propose that specifically the bond of the covenant is love—which Paul called the "bond of perfection" (Col. 3:14).

Two books of the Bible in particular suggest identifying love as the essence of the intra-trinitarian covenant:

---

[1] James Jordan, *The Law of the Covenant*, 5. Emphasis in original.

Deuteronomy and the Gospel of John. As we consider these, we need to remember that the economy reflects the ontology: what God does in the history of creation and redemption shows us who He is in Himself.

Deuteronomy is well-known to be the "covenantal" book *par excellence*. To begin with, Deuteronomy is a group of speeches or sermons that Moses preached on the first day of the eleventh month of the fortieth year after the Exodus, shortly before he died because of the sin that he and Aaron had committed sometime before the fifth month of that same year.[2] But these sermons—which were indeed intended to prepare the sons of Israel for the upcoming conquest of the land that they had refused thirty-eight years previously—are not just pep-talks. Moses' last great work as Israel's prophet was to renew the covenant with the generation that wandered in the wilderness for thiry-eight years after the rebellion at Kadesh Barnea: "These are the words of the covenant which Yahweh commanded Moses to make with the children of Israel in the land of Moab, besides the covenant which He made with them in Horeb" (Deut. 29:1).

Thus, the entire book constitutes a re-statement and renewal of the Sinai covenant in a fuller form than is found in Exodus 20-24 and its "Book of the Covenant" (Exod. 24:7). After writing and preaching the sermons

---

[2] It is profoundly ironic that Moses and Aaron repeated the sin committed by Aaron's sons on the day they were anointed as priests (Lev. 10:1-3). Note the similarity of language: "By those who come near Me I must be regarded as holy" (Lev. 10:3) and "you did not believe in me, to uphold me as holy in the eyes of the people of Israel" (Num. 20:12; cf. Num. 27:14; Deut. 32:51).

of Deuteronomy, Moses commanded the priests to put the "book of Torah" beside the ark of the covenant as a witness against Israel (Deut. 31:26).

Unsurprisingly, therefore, the covenant theme is prominent in Deuteronomy, though it can be said to be prominent throughout the Pentateuch. The word תִּלֹהְב (covenant) appears in Genesis twenty-seven times, in Exodus thirteen times, in Leviticus ten times and in Numbers only five times. Of course, the number of occurrences is not the most important fact, but it still reveals greater emphasis that תִּלֹהְב occurs in Deuteronomy twenty-seven times—the same as Genesis, but about as many times as it occurs from Exodus through Numbers altogether.

The use of the word בהא (love) is also noteworthy. The Hebrew verb for "love" occurs twice in Exodus (20:6; 21:5) and twice also in Leviticus (19:18, 34). It does not appear at all in Numbers. Also, in no occurrence before Deuteronomy does the word "love" ever refer to Yahweh's love for Israel, though of course it must be inferred. There is no doubt that Yahweh's love for Abraham, Isaac, and Jacob is seen in the stories in Genesis or that His love for Israel stands out in the Exodus story, especially, for example, in Exodus 4:22 and in Exodus 19:3-6.

> Thus says Yahweh: 'Israel is My son, My firstborn.'

> Thus you shall say to the house of Jacob, and
>   tell the children of Israel:
> 'You have seen what I did to the Egyptians,
>   and how I bore you on eagles' wings and
>   brought you to Myself.

Now therefore, if you will indeed obey My
voice and keep My covenant,
then you shall be a special treasure to Me
above all people;
for all the earth is Mine.
And you shall be to Me a kingdom of priests
and a holy nation.'
These are the words which you shall speak to
the children of Israel.

Obviously, love does not have to be directly expressed
to be an essential part of a story. Still, the explicit statement of love is significant. In Deuteronomy, the verb בהא
(love) occurs twenty-two times; the feminine noun one
time. Of the twenty-three times the word appears, it refers primarily to Yahweh's love for Israel (4:37; 7:8, 13;
10:15, 18; 23:5) and His command that Israel recipro-
cate (5:10; 6:5; 7:9; 10:12, 19; 11:1, 13, 22; 13:3; 19:9;
30:6, 16, 20). In three verses it refers to love among men.
(15:16; 21:15-16).

The most famous reference among all these is Deuteronomy 6:4-5.

Hear, O Israel: Yahweh our God, Yahweh is
one!
You shall love Yahweh your God
with all your heart, with all your soul, and
with all your strength.

These words cannot be overemphasized.[3] They are Israel's confession of faith in Yahweh, the covenant God—their Father and King. But they include an expression perhaps often not duly noted. I mean the easy-to-overlook phrase "Yahweh our God," which is profoundly important. Consider Exodus 6:7, where this expression sums up the whole of Israel's covenant relationship with God.

> I will take you as My people, and I will be
> your God.
> Then you shall know that I am Yahweh your
> God
> who brings you out from under the burdens of
> the Egyptians.

The words, "I will take you as My people, and I will be your God," define the gracious covenant that God gave to His people Israel. The phrase Yahweh + pronoun (our, your, my) + Elohim, occurs well over six hundred times in the Hebrew Old Testament. In each case, it is an abbreviated but emphatic expression of Yahweh's covenant rela-

---

[3] Contrary to those who would reduce the love command to mere "loyalty" and regard Deuteronomy as a treaty like other ancient Near Eastern treaties—see: William Moran. "The Ancient Near Eastern Background of the Love of God in Deuteronomy," *Catholic Biblical Quarterly* 25 (1963) 77-87—the response Yahweh demanded from Israel called for total devotion of the whole person: inner life, worship, and daily outward works. Whatever distinction one makes between loving Yahweh with "all the heart" and "all the soul," the two expressions together certainly point to the entire inner life of a man, including affection.

tionship with Israel: "I am Yahweh, the Creator God who chose Abraham and his seed to be My special people and I have shown My faithfulness to that covenant by delivering them from Egypt and giving them My covenant at Sinai," or something to that effect. The point is that this short phrase means "covenant relationship," not abstractly, but it terms of redemption from Egypt and the gift of the Torah. That it occurs over six hundred times in the Old Testament is meaningful. But even more noteworthy is the fact that *over three hundred of those occurrences are in the book of Deuteronomy alone!*

Thus, the quintessential covenant book of the Old Testament is also the book of love—Yahweh's love for Israel and a call for Israel to respond to that love. Those who see Torah as a legal relationship—a covenant of works—should take note: the book of Deuteronomy—so influential for the rest of the Old Testament—expounds the covenant as a relationship of love initiated in the grace of Israel's Father-God, Yahweh.

Similarly, in the New Testament, the Gospel of John is also known as a book of love, though it may not be so well-known as a book of the covenant.[4] In Matthew the two most important Greek words for love ἀγαπάω/ἀγάπη and φιλέω are only used fourteen times, in Mark six times, in Luke sixteen times. In the Gospel of John, these words

---

[4] In his *John: Evangelist of the Covenant People: The Narrative and Themes of the Fourth Gospel,* John W. Pryor asserts that "Jesus is presented as Lord of the covenant, reminiscent of Yahweh's status in the Old Testament" (148). He goes on to show the relationship between the Gospel of John and the book of Deuteronomy, especially 148-50, and 157-63.

appear fifty-seven times, including many passages that stand out because of their straightforward teaching about love among the Persons of the Trinity (John 3:35; 5:20; 10:17; 14:31; 15:9-10; 17:23-24, 26).

The portion of John's Gospel that is important for our consideration here is the Upper Room Discourse, from John 13 to 17. Why is that special? Because just as the book of Deuteronomy is Moses' last words to the people of Israel, John 13-17 is the record of Jesus' last pre-resurrection words to the disciples, His last words before the cross.[5] And we know that Jesus is thinking of Deuteronomy here, just like He was when Satan tempted Him and He only responded from Deuteronomy. He knew that like Jacob (Gen. 49) and Moses (Deut. 1-33)—not to mention Joshua (Josh. 24) and David (1 Chron. 28)—His last words had special meaning for the disciples whom He loved as His "little children" (John 13:33). Thus, He borrowed from Moses' definition of love: love is demonstrated, expressed, and manifested in obedience to the commands of Yahweh because the commandments of Yahweh are themselves instruction in the way of love. The following verses are rightly well-known.

---

[5] "Some argue, with some justification, that the book of Deuteronomy provides something of a literary model. Just as Israel is about to enter the promised land, the departing Moses addresses the covenant community; just as Jesus' disciples are about to enter the age of the Spirit, the departing Jesus addresses the new covenant community." Excerpt from D. A. Carson, "The Gospel According to John," Apple Books.

If you love Me, keep My commandments.
    (John 14:15)

He who has My commandments and keeps
    them, it is he who loves Me.
And he who loves Me will be loved by My
    Father,
and I will love him and manifest Myself to
    him. (John 14:21)

Jesus answered and said to him,
If anyone loves Me, he will keep My word;
and My Father will love him,
and We will come to him and make Our home
    with him.
He who does not love Me does not keep My
    words;
and the word which you hear is not Mine but
    the Father's who sent Me.
    (John 14:23-24)

But that the world may know that I love the
    Father,
and as the Father gave Me commandment, so I
    do. Arise, let us go from here.
    (John 14:31)

As the Father loved Me, I also have loved you;
    abide in My love.
If you keep My commandments, you will
    abide in My love,

> just as I have kept My Father's commandments
> and abide in His love. (John 15:9-10)

In His last words to the disciples, Jesus loved them to the end (John 13:1) by teaching them about love: His love for them and His love for the Father.

Throughout the Gospel of John, economy reflects ontology: God gives His Son in covenant love because He is the Triune God of love. John's Gospel repeatedly speaks of the Father's love for the Son (3:35; 5:20; 10:17; 15:9-10; 17:23-24, 26)—far more than it speaks of Jesus' love for the Father (14:31). Jesus' famous prayer emphasizes that the Father's love is eternal: "for You loved Me before the foundation of the world" (John 17:24). The Father's love for the incarnate Son, therefore, reflects the eternal love of the Trinity, and Jesus' obedience to His Father follows the Deuteronomic pattern: love calls for obedience (John 14:15, 21, 23, 24). Jesus is the true Israel who kept Yahweh's covenant and calls for His disciples to do the same: "As the Father loved Me, I also have loved you; abide in My love. If you keep My commandments, you will abide in My love, just as I have kept My Father's commandments and abide in His love" (John 15:9-10).[6]

---

[6] Note: obedience in John's Gospel—indeed in all the Bible—is not blind submission, but the expression of faith and love, which, then, opens the way for and leads to a deeper fellowship of love: "he who loves Me will be loved by My Father, and I will love him and manifest Myself to him" and "If anyone loves Me, he will keep My word; and My Father will love him, and We will come to him and make Our home with him" (John 14:21, 23).

The Father's love for the Son was expressed in the gift of the Spirit at His baptism (John 1:32-34), as the Father declared from heaven, "This is My Son, the beloved, in whom I am well pleased!" (Matt. 3:16-17).[7] He gave the Spirit to Jesus "without measure" (John 3:33-34) because in His love the Father gave "all things" to the Son (John 3:35). Similarly, the Father's love is manifested in showing the Son "all things" that He Himself does (John 5:20). The Father loves the Good Shepherd because He lays down His life for the sheep (John 10:15-18). The Father sent the Son into the world with a mission and Jesus faithfully fulfilled it (John 7:16, 18; 8:26, 29, 42; etc.).

There are, of course, many other places in the Bible that suggest that love is the essential expression of the covenant bond—especially passages showing the relationship between God and His people as a marriage (Hos. 1-3, etc.). The culmination of history is the "bride, the wife of the Lamb," the holy city Jerusalem coming down out of heaven from God, pointing to the biblical story as "deep comedy." The love story that begins with a marriage between Adam and Eve, is abruptly interrupted by the fall into sin, but with redemption in Christ and the gift of the Spirit, the story "can move from death to life," and "history can be redeemed and brought to comic conclusion,"[8] the marriage between the Lamb and the church.

---

[7] For a justification of the translation suggested here, see Ralph Allan Smith, *The Baptism of Jesus the Christ* (Eugene, OR: Wipf & Stock, 2010), 41-48.

[8] Peter J. Leithart, *Deep Comedy: Trinity, Tragedy, and Hope in Western Literature* (Moscow, ID: Canon Press, 2006), xiv.

The economy of history from creation to new creation points to a Triune God of love. In His eternal covenant love, the One True God shares a fellowship of love as the Father loves the Son in the Spirit, and the Son loves the Father in the Spirit, while the Spirit loves the Father in the Son and the Son loves the Spirit in the Father. Each Person is the sphere of love for the other Persons and all share a fellowship of mutual love in their eternal covenantal relationship.[9]

However, having emphasized love as the essence of the covenant, I must add that I am not suggesting that "love" is in some way superior or prior to other attributes of God.[10] All of God's attributes mutually presuppose and include one another. Righteousness must be loving to be truly righteous and love must be righteous, faithful, and good to be truly love. Though love seems to be more emphasized in covenantal passages—especially if חֶסֶד is defined to include "love"—a whole range of attributes

---

[9] As Bosserman states it: "The Father and the Son are related to one another within the personal context of God the Holy Spirit; the Father and the Spirit are related to one another within the personal context of God the Son; and the Son and the Spirit are related to one another within the personal context of God the Father." See: B. A. Bosserman, *The Trinity and the Vindication of Christian Paradox: An Interpretation and Refinement of the Theological Apologetic of Cornelius Van Til* (Eugene, OR: Pickwick Publications, 2014), 179. The whole chapter from which this quote is taken is important, 175ff.

[10] John Frame, *The Doctrine of God* (Phillipsburg, NJ: Presbyterian and Reformed Publishing, 2002), especially chapter 19. See also: Vern S. Poythress, *The Mystery of the Trinity: A Trinitarian Approach to the Attributes of God* (Phillipsburg, NJ: Presbyterian and Reformed Publishing, 2020).

find their proper understanding in the context of God's covenants.[11]

Jordan, therefore, speaks of a "community of life:" Father, Son, and Spirit relating to one another in the abundant richness of all their attributes, each reciprocally giving and receiving according to the distinctives of His individual personhood. The Father is faithful as Father. The Son is kind as Son. The Spirit is generous as the Spirit. The community of life overflows in a dynamic, unrestrained mutual self-giving of each and all to the others. Jordan summarized his view of the bond of the covenant in the following words: "Life is the bond of the covenant, for life is produced by the Spirit, who is the Bond of love in the Trinity."[12]

---

[11] For a fuller discussion of God's attributes and their relation to the covenants, see Ralph A. Smith, *Paradox and Truth: Rethinking Van Til on the Trinity by Comparing Van Til, Plantinga, and Kuyper* (Moscow, ID: Canon Press, 2002), "Covenantal Language and God's Attributes," 81-100.

[12] James Jordan, *Trees and Thorns: Studies in the First Four Chapters of Genesis.* Athanasius Press. Kindle Edition.

CHAPTER 3

THE PRINCIPLE
OF THE COVENANT

This chapter concerns the "principle" of the covenant as it is unfolded in two related concepts: representation and "in-ness." Both in the economy of creation and of redemption, these two ideas are vitally related and should be kept together as the "principle" of the covenant.[1]

---

[1] "Jesus said to him, 'Have I been with you so long, and yet you have not known Me, Philip? He who has seen Me has seen the Father; so how can you say, 'Show us the Father'? Do you not believe that I am in the Father, and the Father in Me? The words that I speak to you I do not speak on My own authority; but the Father who dwells in Me does the works. Believe Me that I am in the Father and the Father in Me, or else believe Me for the sake of the works themselves'" (John 14:9-11). I will return to this later, but it is important enough to emphasize this from the beginning: Jesus can fully represent the Father because He is in the Father and the Father is in Him.

First, consider "representation." As Cornelius Van Til defined it: "It may even be said that Calvin's covenant idea is Theism come to its own. The covenant idea is nothing but the expression of the representational principle consistently applied to all reality."[2] Though Van Til asserts that representation is the principle of the covenant, he does not explain in detail how the idea of representation is related to the covenant, though he does refer to Romans 5:12ff.

To get a fuller picture of the relationship between representation and covenant, we need to take two perspectives into account. One, representation in the covenant history of Abraham and his people, culminating in the Messiah as the new-Adam-representative of the new race of man, illustrates how vital representation is to the covenant idea. Two, even more fundamentally, the doctrine of creation and biblical symbolism show that covenantal representation is fundamental to the structure of the world as created by the Triune God.

We begin, then, with the Abrahamic covenant, for God chose him and his seed to represent mankind before God, in order for them to be a channel of blessing. When Abraham was 99-years-old, Yahweh appeared to him to renew the covenant promise and give Abraham the sign of the covenant—a ceremony for entrance into the covenant (Gen. 17:1-14). Significantly, God makes it clear to Abraham that simply being a physical descendant would not entitle one to the benefits of the covenant. Whoever

---

[2] Excerpt from: Cornelius van Til. "A Survey of Christian Epistemology." Apple Books.

is not circumcised is not a covenant member, no matter who his physical ancestors may be (Gen 17:14).

The promise that Abraham would be a "father of a multitude of nations" and that "kings will come from you" (Gen. 17:5-6) was essentially repeated also to Sarah (17:16). Circumcision, in other words, was the sign of the covenant promise that Yahweh had made to Abraham when He originally called him: "I will make you a great nation; I will bless you. And make your name great; And you shall be a blessing. I will bless those who bless you, And I will curse him who curses you; And in you all the families of the earth shall be blessed." Abraham was chosen to bring blessing to the world. Through him the curses of Eden and Babel would be removed and God would fulfill His covenant plan for mankind.

In the story of Joseph, this begins to be fulfilled in a public manner that was also prophetic. Joseph, as a type of Christ, "died" and was "buried" in an Egyptian prison, but was raised from that death and seated at the right hand of power to bring salvation to the sons of Israel and also the nations. The seed of Abraham brought salvation to the world. Then, we see the meaning of the Abrahamic covenant even more fully in Israel's redemption from Egypt. Yahweh brought the children of Israel to Mt. Sinai "on eagles' wings" (Ex. 19:4) so that He could give them His covenant and make them a special treasure to Himself—a kingdom of priests, a holy nation. It is by being priestly representatives of the nations that Israel would bring the Abrahamic blessing!

Consider the covenant law and how it sets forth the representative principle. At Sinai, the notion of representation that was implicit in the Abrahamic covenant becomes a fully articulated principle, for, among other things, priests are representatives of others. This representative status of the whole nation found particular expression in the feast of Tabernacles when Israel sacrificed seventy bulls in prayer for the nations of the world (Num. 29:12-38): Abraham's representative seed blessing the families of the earth.

However, though all the children of Israel were priests, that did not mean everyone had equal access to all priestly privileges, as the story of Korah's rebellion shows (Num. 16:1-40). Even though Korah was a member of the tribe of Levi and had special access to a degree, he was not from the family of Aaron. Only ordained descendants of Aaron could draw near to God in the tabernacle. And even among them, only the high priest could function as supreme representative of the people. Among other things, the high priest's representative status was defined by the onyx stones on his shoulders with the names of the tribes of Israel written on them and by his breastplate with a stone for each tribe (Exod. 39:1-21).

Also, every animal sacrificed functioned as a representative, for the offerer laid his hands on the animal to signify that the sacrifice was his substitute and representative, ascending to God in his place. As Leithart explains:

> Worshipers themselves do not draw near to
> Yahweh's table to offer themselves as "bread"
> for God (see lehem 'ĕlōhîm, Lev 21:21-22).
> They send animals to act as priest on their be-
> half. Worshipers do not pass by the cherubim

in their own persons, but send substitutionary animals to represent them in Yahweh's presence, to submit to the sword and to be translated to divine smoke and fire on their behalf.[3]

The priestly status of the circumcised nation—fully expressed in the system of priests, festivals, and sacrifices—provides rich background for the meaning of the Messiah as the covenant representative of Israel and head of a new race of mankind.[4] Jesus fulfilled Israel's calling: In

---

[3] Leithart, *Delivered from the Elements*, 106. In a footnote on the same page, Leithart adds: "The claim that the sacrificial animal is a 'substitute' is hotly controversial, but incontrovertible when the Levitical system is placed within its narrative context. The sacrificial system assumes exile from Eden; the worshiper approaches a God who is enthroned behind a screen of cherubic guardians with swords of fire. The worshiper cannot draw near without dying; so he sends an animal ahead on his behalf. The animal is sent to bring the worshiper into God's presence; the animal dies and is turned to smoke, and the worshiper remains quite alive and nonsmoky. The only word that fits what happens is 'substitute.' It is important to recognize the 'inclusive' character of the substitution: the animal does what the worshiper cannot do, but he does it so that, represented by the animal, the worshiper himself can have his sins covered and can draw near. Further, the Aqedah and Passover stand behind the sacrificial system: every worshiper is Abraham offering Isaac, and every sacrifice reenacts the deliverance of Passover. In both cases, an animal took the place of a human, a son, who was in danger, and the animal died in place of the son."

[4] See, Matthew W. Bates, *The Birth of the Trinity: Jesus, God, and Spirit in New Testament and Early Christian Interpretations of the Old Testament* (Oxford: Oxford University Press, 2015), especially the discussion of Isaiah 42:1-9, 96-101. See also, Grant Macaskill, who

Jesus, God himself lived a human life *in* flesh that was not controlled *by* flesh. He came into flesh by an act of the Spirit, and so while in the flesh he lived the life of the Spirit. Thus Jesus is the true Israelite, the Davidic king, doing what Yahweh required every Israelite and every king of Israel to do, living according to Torah while in flesh. As Davidic king, Jesus embodies Israel; as just Davidic king, Jesus embodies the *just* Israel that Yahweh always wanted and promised. It is the kind of life that Torah's antisarkic regimen always aimed to produce.[5]

Jesus the high priest of the new covenant appeared in the heavenly holy place as a representative and mediator for all who are called (Heb. 9:11-15). In place of circumcision as the ceremony to enter the covenant, Christians are circumcised with a circumcision made without hands

---

also brings representation and "in-ness" together: "This covenantal framework must serve as the starting point for reflection on participation or union with Christ. That starting point must involve a recognition that, as the Elect One, the Messiah, Jesus is the covenant representative. His life and death are doubly significant in covenant terms. Born 'under the law', he fulfils the conditions and takes the curse of the old covenant, and his blood serves to ratify the new covenant. . . . To be united to Jesus, to be in him, is to be in the covenant through his representative headship. Thus, it is to be in a condition of covenantal communion with God, with the covenant-fulfilment of Jesus serving as the grounds for our own communion. In Christ, we keep the covenant." *Union with Christ in the New Testament* (Oxford: Oxford University Press, 2013), 298.

[5] Leithart, *Delivered from the Elements,* 136.

when they are buried and raised with Christ in baptism (Col. 2:11-12). Just as circumcision placed the descendants of Abraham "into" the covenant, baptism inserts the Christian "into" Christ (Rom. 6:3; Gal. 3:27). But baptism does far more than circumcision, for baptism is also ordination into the priesthood, and that means that every Christian can not only offer the sacrifice of praise and thanksgiving, but we all have access to the most holy place in heaven (Heb. 13:15; 4:16; 10:19-25).[6]

The baptized body of Christ is a new priesthood, offering new sacrifices. Who do we represent? We represent the body as a whole, for each of us brings praise and prayer for the whole body. But we also come before God to offer ourselves as living sacrifices to serve God and the world (Rom. 12:1). Moreover, the church represents the world outside of Christ in prayer and worship to bring the world unto God (cf. John 17:18, 21, 23),[7] fulfilling

---

[6] See Peter J. Leithart, *The Priesthood of the Plebs: A Theology of Baptism* (Eugene, OR: Wipf and Stock Publishers, 2003). Leithart argues "that baptism fulfills and replaces the ordination rite and therefore has the same role in the church as ordination had in Israel, namely consecrating priests for ministry in God's house." We may add that in so far as baptism unites us with the Messiah, it also anoints us as kings and prophets (Acts 2:17-18; 1 Pet. 2:9; Rev. 1:6; 5:10; 20:6; etc.)

[7] Leithart's insight on Christian worship is relevant here: "When Hebrews exhorts us to offer a continuous 'sacrifice of praise' (Hebrews 13:15), we instinctively think "sacrifice" is a metaphor. Real sacrifice, we assume, needs blood, flesh, altars, and smoke. That instinct gets things exactly backwards. Think about Jesus. Jesus offers the true, human sacrifice that atones for sin once-for-all. His blood does what the blood of bulls and goats could never do. We should apply the same logic to our liturgical 'sacrifices.' According to Scripture, the old sacrifices were shadows, faint images of true. What we do is the

the promise of the Abrahamic covenant: "All the families of the earth shall be blessed."

The other perspective on representation is, as I said, more fundamental, but in some ways may be more difficult to understand, at least for Christians in our day. I am speaking of biblical symbolism. In words repeated twice in his essay, James Jordan says: "*Symbolism is more important than anything else for the life of man.*"[8] Jordan adds: "Anyone who does not understand this has yet to fully come to grips with the philosophy of Cornelius Van Til, or more importantly, with the biblical doctrine of creation."[9]

Jordan explains this as follows:

> The doctrine of creation means that every created item, and also the created order as a whole, *reflects* the character of the God who created it. In other words, everything in the creation, and the creation as a whole, points to God. In short, *everything is a sign or symbol of God.* The idea that everything is a symbol of God, His character, nature, ways, etc., is the foundation stone of the philosophy of Cornelius Van Til.

---

reality that Israel's symbolic sacrifices pointed to. In worship, we offer ourselves as living sacrifices in Jesus. Everything that happened symbolically in Old Testament sacrifice happens in Spirit and truth in Christian song." Blog post on Facebook, October 19, 2021: https://www.facebook.com/Leithart/

[8] James B. Jordan, *Symbolism: A Manifesto*, https://biblicalhorizons.com/wp-content/uploads/2017/12/Symbolism-A-Manifesto.pdf

[9] Ibid.

The doctrine of creation *ex nihilo* is the basis of the Vantillian doctrine of natural revelation.[10]

Just as the whole creation is a symbol of the Triune God who created all things, man is His special symbol, His living image. One of the things that distinguishes man from other symbols is that man, as God's special image, is himself a symbol maker. However radically men may deny God, they will still fulfill, in a perverse way, their calling as symbol makers—in art, literature, music, philosophy. Man cannot escape being the image of God.

As Jordan pointed out above, revelation—both in the created world and in Scripture—is grounded in the representational principle, though he does not use that term. All creation represents God as symbols of who He is in His Trinitarian glory. This is fundamental to the biblical worldview, as it is presented to us in the Bible, as Jordan wrote:

> The Biblical worldview is not given to us in the discursive and analytical language of philosophy and science, but in the rich and compact language of symbolism and art. It is pictured in ritual and architecture, in numerical structures and geographical directions, in symbols and types, in trees and stars. In short, it is given to us in a premodern package that seems at places very strange.[11]

---

[10] Ibid.

[11] *Through New Eyes* (Brentwood, TN: Wolgemuth & Hyatt, 1989), 1.

Jordan's book, *Through New Eyes*, as well as his biblical commentaries on Judges[12] and Daniel,[13] lectures on Revelation and other books of the Bible,[14] show how understanding biblical symbolism enables a reader to enter the biblical worldview and read the Bible "through new eyes." The theological ground and source for this is the fact that the Persons of the Trinity are mutually representative. The ontology of Father, Son, and Spirit as a God of covenant love and fellowship underlies the symbolism of creation and the verbal revelation given to us in the Word—both incarnate and written.

These two perspectives on representation show that this principle of the covenant is pervasive and prominent. We turn now to the other and related aspect of the principle of the covenant: "in-ness," a concept no less important, but perhaps not as well-known. I begin again with Abraham and the promise to him, which is reiterated with emphasis, that the nations would be blessed "in" him (Gen. 12:3; 18:18; 22:18; 26:4). This great covenant promise in Genesis is picked up by Paul, who says that Scripture preached the gospel to Abraham in the words "in you shall all the nations be blessed," explaining further that it is "in Christ" that the blessing of Abraham comes to the Gentiles (Gal. 3:8-14).

---

[12] *Judges: God's War Against Humanism* (Tyler, TX: Geneva Ministries, 1985).

[13] *The Handwriting on the Wall: A Commentary on the Book of Daniel* (Powder Springs, GA: American Vision, 2007).

[14] For Jordan's lectures, see James B. Jordan (Theopolis Institute), Theopolis app, https://app.theopolisinstitute.com/

Though it may not be clear in the Genesis account, Paul tells us that all people are naturally "in Adam" through physical birth, fleshly descendants who must die: "in Adam all die" (1 Cor. 15:22). This is a fundamental "old" covenant truth. In the new covenant, believers are baptized "into Christ"[15] (Gal. 3:27; Rom. 6:3), with the result that they are "in" Christ: "Therefore, if anyone is in Christ, he is a new creation; old things have passed away; behold, all things have become new" (2 Cor. 5:17). Gal. 3:27 explicitly connects the themes of "in-ness" with representation and priesthood: baptism places the Christian "into Christ" and also clothes him with Christ. In other words, Christ Himself is the priestly garment for the new covenant believer.[16]

Though brief—a full study would require an entire volume—the discussion above should suffice to show that Van Til's assertion that representation is the principle of the covenant is biblical. It also shows that the notion of "in-ness" is vitally related to covenant membership and representation. Thus, in the economy of salvation, representation and "in-ness" function as two aspects of a

---

[15] Or, "into" the Name: "baptizing them into the name [εἰς τὸ ὄνομα] of the Father, and of the Son, and of the Holy Spirit" (Matt. 28:19). D. A. Carson has: "Those who become disciples are to be baptized *eis* (NIV text note, "into") the name of the Trinity. Matthew, unlike some NT writers, apparently avoids the confusion of *eis* (strictly "into") and *en* (strictly "in"; cf. Zerwick, *Biblical Greek*, para. 106) common in Hellenistic Greek; if so, the preposition "into" strongly suggests a coming-into-relationship-with or a coming-under-the-lordship-of (cf. Allen; Albright and Mann)." Excerpt from *Matthew* (The Expositor's Bible Commentary), iBooks.

[16] *Delivered from the Elements*, 102-108.

fundamental covenant principle. How does this reflect or manifest the ontology?

It is worth returning to Van Til here:

> The foundation of the representational princi-
> ple among men is the fact that the Trinity exists
> in the form of a mutually exhaustive represen-
> tation of the three Persons that constitute it. . . .
> It was upon this foundation of a truly trinitar-
> ian concept that Calvin built his conception of
> covenant theology. If the Persons of the Trinity
> are representationally exhaustive of one anoth-
> er, human thought is cast on representational
> lines too. There would in that case be no other
> than a completely personalistic atmosphere in
> which human personality could function. Ac-
> cordingly, when man faced any fact whatsoever,
> he would ipso facto be face to face with God.[17]

In what sense do the Persons of the Trinity represent one another? This can be seen most simply and clearly in the economy. Jesus represented the Father to men: for no man has seen God at any time, but the "only begotten Son, who is in the bosom of the Father, He has declared Him." Jesus represented the Father so perfectly and whol-ly that He could say to Philip, "He who has seen Me has seen the Father" (John 14:9). Jesus explains this further when He says that He is "in" the Father and the Father is

---

[17] Excerpt from: Cornelius van Til. "A Survey of Christian Episte-mology." Apple Books.

"in" Him (John 14:11). Later in the same Upper Room Discourse, Jesus tells the disciples that He will send the Holy Spirit to be with them and even "in" them, for the Spirit is sent to represent Jesus to the disciples (John 14:16-18; 14:26; 15:26-27; 16:7-15).

Although Jesus' representing the Father and the Spirit's representing Jesus are examples of Trinitarian Persons representing one another in the economy of salvation, they clearly point to the expressly declared ontology: "He [the Son] is the brightness of the glory and the exact imprint of His [the Father's] person (or "nature" or "being," Greek: ὑπόστασις.)" From eternity past, the Son represented the Father as His express image and the reflection of His glory.

Thus, the Son was the only Person who could be chosen to reveal God in the economy. From eternity He was, and now also is, the reflection of the Father Himself, a reflection of the Father to the Father, a mirror of the Father's Person that the Father sees through the Spirit—for just as it is in and through the Spirit that God is revealed in the economy (1 Cor. 2:10-11), it must also be so in the Trinitarian ontology. The Father appointed the Son and the Spirit to represent Him to the world because they represent Him in the intra-trinitarian ontology.

Here it is important to more fully consider the subject of "in-ness," which we previously saw was part of the whole notion of representation. Jesus could claim to be the perfect representative of the Father—"He who has seen Me has seen the Father"—because the Father is "in" Him and He is "in" the Father. The idea that the Persons of the Trinity mutually indwell one another is essential to trinitarian theology and is called "perichoresis."[18]

The Father, Son, and Spirit indwell one another absolutely and perfectly, so that all that the Father is belongs to the Son and the Spirit—except His fatherhood—and all that the Son and Spirit are belong to each other and to the Father—except their personal distinctives. The mutually indwelling Persons—Father, Son, and Spirit—are fully One. The idea that the Three are exhaustively representative of one another and fully "in" one another expresses the covenantal ontology of the Father, Son, and Spirit. To stress the point again: covenant in the Triune God is not an "agreement" or "contract." It is a relationship of mutual representation and indwelling, especially manifested in the eternal self-giving love of Father, Son, and Spirit.

Because they fully indwell one another, they share all attributes, though they "inflect" them in a distinct manner, according to the Person. Explaining Athanasius, Leithart writes:

---

[18] "Perichoresis means 'mutual indwelling,' or 'reciprocal penetration,' and describes the exhaustive mutual indwelling of the persons of the Trinity, the mystery of the Father's being in the Son that is eternally simultaneous with the Son's indwelling of the Father, and their mutual dwelling in the Spirit." Peter J. Leithart, *Traces of the Trinity: Signs of God in Creation and Human Experience*. Baker Publishing Group. Kindle Edition. The subtitle of Leithart's book deserves emphasis: there are "signs" of the Triune God in the created world and in our daily human experience because all creation symbolizes God and the children of Adam are His special symbol.

On another interpretation, Athanasius is saying that the Father has 'his own' wisdom, but that wisdom is paternal wisdom, which means wisdom that exists in the Father (*ad se*) only as it is the wisdom poured out for and manifest in the Son. The Son too has 'his own' wisdom, but has that wisdom only as receptive wisdom, received eternally from the Father. Each of the persons shares all the same attributes, and these attributes are their 'own,' but these attributes are 'inflected' relationally, 'held' by each person distinctly as a person. All the Father's attributes are inflected paternally, the Son's filially, the Spirit's spiritually.[19]

Also, it is because the Three indwell one another so perfectly and wholly, indwell one another without reserve, that we must say that God is One. God's Oneness is not prior to His Threeness or His Threeness prior to His Oneness. The three mutually indwelling Persons *are* the One God. There is no substratum of "Being" underneath them in which or through which they are united.

This deserves some attention. Explaining Aquinas' view of the Trinity, Perez wrote,

---

[19] Peter Leithart, *Athanasius*, 77. The quotation above represents one interpretation of Athanasius' view and not the interpretation that Leithart favors. Whether or not it is the correct interpretation of Athanasius, I believe it is a profound statement of God's attributes considered in the light of the Trinity.

The persons are not prior to the relations. The persons are constituted by the relations. There is not a pre-existing substrate for gift and relation. They are in so far as they are reciprocally relative. Relation unites and distinguishes at the same time. The unity of God is not that of a solitary, but that of a perfect communion. The being of God is identified with relation, and is an eternal exchange of love: relation, in so far as it is a divine reality, is the essence itself. God's being is love. This presupposes a co-dignity of the three persons; a same love that is possessed in a different manner by each of them; it also presupposes distinction. With Thomas Aquinas it is absolutely clear that there is no pre-existing substrate of the Father, the Son and the Holy Spirit, whose being is reciprocal gift or communion in love.[20]

I remember reading of a Christian minister who preached on Trinity Sunday and illustrated the doctrine of the Trinity by asking his congregation to imagine a father, mother, and child in bed together. The father obviously points to the Father and the child to the Son. The mother in this illustration is the Holy Spirit. But the minister also explained that the bed was the "Being" of God! Using no illustration would have been much better

---

[20] Ángel Cordovilla Pérez, "The Trinitarian Concept of Person" in, Giulio Maspero and Robert J. Woźniak ed., *Rethinking Trinitarian Theology: Disputed Questions and Contemporary Issues in Trinitarian Theology* (London: T&T Clark, 2012), 122.

than an illustration suggesting that the Trinity is actually a "Four"—three Persons + one Being.

William G. T. Shedd, not uniquely, explicitly denies that the Trinity is a "four:" "Again, when it is said that there are three persons in one essence, it is not meant that the essence is a fourth thing, within which the three persons exist." He labors to express himself clearly: "From eternity, divine essence subsists in a trinal manner. The instant that it is one essence, it is three persons. To conceive of it as a mere monad, marked by singleness, is erroneous."[21]

Thomas Weinandy's explanation is even better. He expresses the mystery of the Trinity in this way:

> The being of God (I prefer the expression 'the being of God' to the phrase 'the substance of God') *is* the Trinity which is the one act of the Father begetting the Son and spirating the Spirit. The eternal constituting of the persons takes place within (and not outside of) the one being of God and therefore is the one being of God. There is neither priority of oneness nor of threeness. Three persons *are* one God or one God *is* three persons."[22]

---

[21] Excerpt from: William G. T. Shedd. "Dogmatic Theology." Apple Books.

[22] Thomas Weinandy, *The Father's Spirit of Sonship: Reconceiving the Trinity* (Eugene, OR: Wipf and StockPublishers, 1995), 64. Walter Kasper uses similar language speaking of the Greek approach to the Trinity: "The Greeks start with the hypostases and understand the perichoresis as an active reciprocal penetration; the perichoresis is as

Though the word "perichoresis" does not appear in this quotation, Weinandy is expounding his understanding of the implications of the mutual indwelling of the Persons of the Trinity.

Similarly, Thomas Torrance wrote:

> The distinctively Christian conceptions of "person" and of "being" in the doctrine of God (applied to divine Being in a unique way and to human being in a creaturely way) arose together, each bearing decisively on the other. God was now known and worshipped and glorified as a fullness of Personal Being in himself, indeed as himself a transcendent *Communion of Persons*, for the three divine Persons, Father, the Son and the Holy Spirit are the One God. With God, Being and Communion are one and the same. The theological concept of the Being of God as used, for example, in the formula "One Being, Three Persons" (*mia ousia, tres upostasis*) agreed at the Council of Alexandria presided over by Athanasius in AD 362, is not to be understood as referring to three Persons *in* God's Being as if the three Persons were other than and not identical with the one Being of God, but precisely as the One Being of God. Hence the Being of God was not understood in terms of any preconceived idea or definition

---

it were the bond uniting the persons." Excerpt from Kasper, Walter. "God of Jesus Christ: New Edition." Apple Books.

of divine Being, but exclusively in the light of God's naming of himself as "I am who I am" in the Old Testament revelation and as the Father, the Son and the Holy Spirit in the New Testament revelation, as in the dominical formula for Holy Baptism. Within this New Testament revelation the Old Testament self-naming of God as "I am" was taken up in the "I am" of the Lord Jesus Christ in whom as the very off-spring of God's Nature and in his Spirit God has made himself more fully known to us in the personal Communion which his own Being is. Thus in the doctrine of the Holy Trinity the one Being of God who is three Persons, does not refer to some abstract essence, but, as noted above, to the intensely personal "I am" of God, the eternal living Being that God is of himself as the Father, the Son and the Holy Spirit, and so as intrinsically triune and intrinsically personal. The divine Being and the divine Communion are to be understood wholly in terms of one another.[23]

---

[23] Thomas F. Torrance, *The Christian Doctrine of God, One Being, Three Persons* (London: Bloomsbury, T & T Clark, 2016), 104. Following a discussion of God's covenant with Israel, Torrance writes: "Although the specific concept of 'person' and of the 'personal' had not yet arisen, the coupling of the 'I am' of *Yahweh* and the 'I am' of our Lord together gave rise, as we have seen, during the formulation of the doctrine of the Trinity, to an onto-relational and fully personal conception of the Being of God, and indeed to the understanding of the Being of God as Communion, for the three divine Persons in their Communion with one another *are* the Triune Being of God, and there

In the economy, indwelling, like the indwelling of Yahweh in the tabernacle and temple, is a covenantal truth. Yahweh's presence was presence as the Lord of the covenant people, the very heart of their covenant relationship. In the same way, the indwelling of the Spirit of God in Christians makes us temples of God, sanctified by His covenant presence. The ectypal picture points to the archetype from which it derives: the covenantal ontology of the mutually indwelling Persons of the Trinity. Perichoresis in the Trinity is both ontological and covenantal—what Torrance calls "onto-relational." Or, to state it in different terms, perichoresis is the ontological expression of the covenantal bond which joins the Persons of the Trinity in a community of life. Thus, too, the principle of the covenant, found in the interrelated notions of representation and in-ness—both aspects of God's Trinitarian covenant life—is expressed in the covenants that the Triune God gives to His people.

---

is no other God but he who is Father, Son and Holy Spirit," 124.

CHAPTER 4

THE STRUCTURE
OF THE COVENANT

In his study of covenant sequences in the books of Leviticus and Deuteronomy, James Jordan wrote:

> The Bible reveals that God's way of managing history is by making covenants with His people. There is a succession of such covenants in the Bible, each more glorious than the previous, each absorbing and transfiguring the previous, until finally we come to the New Covenant in Jesus Christ."[1]

---

[1] James B. Jordan, *Covenant Structure in Leviticus and Deuteronomy* (Tyler, TX: Institute for Christian Economics, 1989), 3.

From Adam to Christ, God only related to mankind through covenants. The first two covenants, the covenant with Adam and the covenant with Noah, were covenants with the whole human race. In fact, the covenant with Noah explicitly included the animals (Gen. 9:9-17), which presupposes that the original covenant relationship with Adam in the garden also included the animals. Subsequent covenants focused especially on redemption from sin with the aim of building the kingdom of God. They were made with Abraham, the people of Israel through Moses, David, and with post-exilic Judah in the days of Ezra.[2] The final covenant, as Jordan pointed out, is the New Covenant in Jesus.

All of these covenants share structural features, but in speaking of "structure," Jordan is not describing covenants in a wooden or mechanical manner. Structure does not imply "static." When Jordan suggests various approaches to the structure of biblical covenants, he says:

> There is a sequence of items that is found in biblical covenants. The overall sequence is almost always the same. There are also in the Bible various ways of grouping this sequence, according to symbolically significant numbers. Scholars have identified groups of three (Trinity), four (world foundations), five (housebuilding), six (man), and seven (sabbath). We might

[2] In part four of his work *Through New Eyes*, Jordan details the succession of covenants under the title "The Movement of History." James B. Jordan, *Through New Eyes* (Brentwood, TN: Wolgemuth & Hyatt, 1989), 167-289.

profitably also look for groups of ten (law) and twelve (covenant people). There seems to be a certain prominence to the five-fold arrangement in the Pentateuch, with its five books, perhaps because five is a number associated with housebuilding."[3]

The overall sequence that Jordan is referring to above can be described as a "flow" almost as accurately as it can be a "structure."[4] Note how fluid and broad the categories are as Jordan describes the covenant in the following twelve aspects, each of which in one way or another exhibits the dynamic nature of God's covenantal relationships.

1. Announcement of God's transcendence; His laying hold of the situation (Exod. 2:24-25; 20:3).

---

[3] Ibid., 6. George Mendenhall's groundbreaking work, *Law and Covenant in Israel and the Ancient Near East* (Biblical Colloquium; Pittsburgh, PA: Presbyterian Board of Colportage of Western Pennsylvania, 1955) gave birth to a whole industry of studies on the relationship between the covenant idea in the Bible and the cultures of the Ancient Near East. Meredith Kline, K. A. Kitchen, Jeffrey J. Niehaus, are among the many whose studies show that biblical covenants have structures similar to covenants in other societies. However, as I pointed out previously, most of these scholars use the ANE as background for the Bible, rather than seeing the Bible as the background for the ANE. Jordan's approach to the structure of the covenant is unique in that he takes the Bible as his starting point and describes the covenant relationship in a much fuller form, as the twelve aspects above show. Most importantly, as his definition indicates, "covenant" for Jordan is first of all a Trinitarian idea, or, rather, a living Trinitarian reality.

[4] Think of how quantum mechanics describes an electron.

2. Declaration of God's new Name, appropriate for the new covenant being installed (Exod. 3:13-15; 6:2-8; 20:2a).

3. Statement of how God brought His people from the old covenant and world into the new one (Exod. 20:2b; Deut. 1:6-4:40).

4. Establishment of the new covenant order, especially the governmental hierarchies thereof (Exod. 18:13-27; Deut. 1:9-18).

5. Appointment of new names for the new finished product (Gen. 1:4-5, 6-8, 9-10; at Moses' time, 'children of Israel' is the new name, replacing 'Hebrew').

6. Grant or distribution of an area of dominion to the covenant steward or vassal (Exod. 3:8; Deut. 1:19-12:31).

7. Stipulations concerning the management of this grant (Exod. 20-23; Deut. 5:1-26:19).

8. Statement of the terms by which God will evaluate man's performance: promised blessings and threatened curses (Exod. 23:25-33; Deut. 27, 28).

9. Placement of witnesses to report to God on man's behavior (Ex. 23:20-23; Deut. 4:26; 30:19).

10. Arrangements for the deposition of the covenant documents (Exod. 40:20; Deut. 31:9-13).

11. Arrangements for succession of covenant vice-regents (Deut. 31:7, 14, 23; Deut. 34).

12. Artistic poems that encapsulate the covenant, and that are to be taught to succeeding generations (Deut. 31:14-33:29).[5]

Keeping in mind that Jordan's concern is with biblical covenants that God has given to man, two things that Jordan stresses bear repetition. First, covenant documents generally reflect the sequence of events in the making of a covenant. God is managing history, leading it to a goal in an orderly process. From the time of Moses, He reveals His covenants in documents. Second, though commandments and laws are a feature of every covenant, covenants are a gift of God's grace. There is no grace versus law tension in biblical covenants, including the Mosaic covenant.

The "structure" indicated in the twelve aspects of a covenant is somewhat ambiguous. However, it is clear enough to consider God's covenant making activity throughout the history of redemption. The important thing to note is that covenants in the Bible come to documentary expression in such a structured form. Since the covenant document is given by God and is structured by the events in the process of God's giving the covenant, in looking at covenant structures, we are considering the way that God typically works in history.

That takes us back to what we called the "foundation" of the idea that there is a covenantal relationship among the Persons of the Trinity: the economy reflects the ontology. If the economy reflects the ontology and covenantal relationships in the economy are "structured," we are led

---

[5] Ibid., 4.

to consider the "structure" of Trinitarian relationships. Is there anything like a "structure" in God's intra-trinitarian relationships?

Classic trinitarian theology does describe a "structure" in the relationships among the Three Persons. Primarily, though not exclusively, upon the basis of the baptismal formula—"in the name of the Father, and of the Son, and of the Holy Spirit"—we say that the Father is the First Person, the Son is the Second Person, and the Spirit is the Third Person. The order suggested is linear, following the names of the Persons—names which imply their mutual relationships. The Father is Father of the Son from eternity, in essence. There was never a time that the Father was not Father. He cannot not be Father. In the same way, the Son has always been and cannot not be the Son. The Father and the Son spirate (breathe out) the Spirit. Neither Father nor Son can be Father or Son without the Spirit of Life. Though His name is admittedly less perspicuous, the eternal Spirit is not less necessary to the life of the One God than are Father or Son.

The Father-Son relationship is complicated by the fact that the Greek word μονογενής may be translated "only begotten" or "only," depending on how one understands the word. But however one understands the Greek word, there are more fundamental considerations, as William G. T. Shedd explains:

> Some trinitarians have attempted to hold the doctrine of the Trinity while denying eternal generation, spiration, and procession. They concede that there are three eternal persons in

the Godhead, denominated in Scripture Father, Son, and Spirit, but contend that to go beyond this and affirm such acts in the Godhead as generation and spiration is to go beyond the record. They reject, or at least doubt, this feature in Nicene trinitarianism.

But this is inconsistent. These trinal names Father, Son, and Spirit, given to God in Scripture, force upon the theologian the ideas of paternity, filiation, spiration, and procession. He cannot reflect upon the implication of these names without forming these ideas and finding himself necessitated to concede their literal validity and objective reality. He cannot say with Scripture that the first person is the Father and then deny or doubt that he "fathers." He cannot say that the second person is the Son and then deny or doubt that he is "begotten." He cannot say that the third person is the Spirit and then deny or doubt that he "proceeds" by "spiration" (Spirit because spirated) from the Father and Son. Whoever accepts the nouns Father, Son, and Spirit as conveying absolute truth must accept also the corresponding adjectives and predicates—beget and begotten, spirate and proceed—as conveying absolute truth.[6]

---

[6] William G. T. Shedd, *Dogmatic Theology*, ed. Alan W. Gomes, 3rd ed. (Phillipsburg, NJ: P & R Publishing, 2003), 245.

What Shedd refers to is expressed in traditional Trinitarian theology as "ingenerate" (the Father), "generation" (the Son), and "spiration" (the Spirit).[7] The Father Himself is not "derived" from any. The Son and the Spirit are "derived" from the Father.[8] The Father generates the Son and spirates (breathes out) the Spirit with and through the Son.

In speaking of the Father generating the Son—as the Niceno-Constantinopolitan Creed (381) does, "And in one Lord Jesus Christ, the only-begotten Son of God, begotten of the Father before all worlds, Light of Light, very God of very God, begotten, not made, consubstantial with the Father"—Christians are specifically denying the "Arian"[9] claim that there was a time when the Son

---

[7] In Bavinck's words: "(1) paternity ('unbegottenness,' active generation, and active spiration); (2) filiation or sonship, passive generation, active spiration; (3) procession or passive spiration." Excerpt from: Herman Bavinck. "Reformed Dogmatics Volume 2: God and Creation." Apple Books.

[8] The Father is the "source" of the Son, otherwise He would not eternally be the Father, but that does not mean or suggest ontological subordination. On the contrary, as Athanasius argued, the Son's generation from the Father implies that He is equal to the Father. Leithart, *Athanasius,* 51-52.

[9] Leithart notes: "As Rowan Williams declares in his review of Hanson, 'the time has probably come to relegate the term Arianism at least to inverted commas, and preferably to oblivion.'" The complications surrounding a correct historical understanding of Arius and Arianism, the extended Trinitarian controversies of the Fourth Century, and the subtle difficulties surrounding terminology perhaps render the word "Arianism" an unhelpful term in academic discussion. But I think, depending on the context, it still serves a function. Leithart, *Athanasius,* 179-80. For the continued use of the word "Arianism," see 17.

was not.[10] The "begetting" being referred to is eternal, just as the Father and the Son are eternal. Without the Son, the Father would not be the Father and without being eternally begotten of the Father, the Son would not be the Son.

This language suggests order and structure in the relationships between Father, Son, and Spirit, but the order is not necessarily a simple linear one. In his comments on Revelation 1:4-5—where the order is Father, Spirit, Son—Peter Leithart writes:

> We may reason from the economy to the ontology. According to Scripture and the creeds, the Father eternally begets the Son; the Son is the "only-begotten of the Father" (Jn. 1:14). If the incarnation reveals the relation of Father and Son, we may say that the Father eternally begets the Son through the Spirit. The Spirit is the Love by which the Father begets the Son, the Love

---

10 Anthony Hoekema describes the Jehovah's Witnesses as Arians, though he notes there are a number of important differences between the modern cult and the ancient heresy. "Essentially, the Jehovah-Witness view of the person of Christ is a revival of the Arian heresy of the fourth century AD. Arius (who lived from approximately A.D. 280 to 336) and his followers (called Arians) taught that the Son, whom they also called the Logos or Word, had a beginning, that the term *beget* when applied to the generation of the Son meant to *make*, and that therefore the Son was not of the same substance as the Father but was a creature who had been called into existence by the Father. The Arians taught that there was a time when God was alone and was not yet a Father. Arius went on to ascribe to Christ only a subordinate, secondary, created divinity." Anthony A. Hoekema, *Jehovah's Witnesses* (Grand Rapids: Eerdmans, 1963), 122.

through which the Son loves the Father. The Spirit is the breath by which the Father generates the Son who will become Last Adam. Since the Father is the Father only because he has a Son, the Spirit through whom the Father begets the Son makes the Father Father, even as, being the agent of begetting, he makes the Son Son. Through the Spirit who proceeds from Father and Son, Father and Son receive their personal properties and relations, as Father and Son. Father, Spirit, Son highlights the ontological Trinity as a communion of mutually dependent Persons.[11]

Leithart adds a quotation from Thomas Weinandy:

The Son is Son because, having been begotten by the Father in the Spirit of sonship, he loves the Father as the Son. This act of filial love, enacted in the Spirit of sonship, is what makes him the Son. This means that the Father is the Father not only because he begets the Son, but also because, in the begetting of the Son, the Son loves the Father, and so as Son helps constitute the Father as Father. The Father would not be Father unless he had a Son who loved him as Son. Now the cornerstone which holds together this fatherly act of lovingly begetting the Son and this filial

---

[11] Peter J. Leithart, *Revelation 1-11* (London: Bloomsbury T & T Clark, 2018), 86.

act of the Son loving the Father is provided by the action of the Spirit.[12]

In the Father's eternal begetting of the Son, and the Father's and the Son's eternal spirating of the Spirit, the three Persons of the Trinity in their perichoretic fellowship of love share the structured bond of covenant life. The Father and the Son love one another in the Spirit, who pours out their mutual love in the ontological Trinity, just as He pours out the love of God upon us in the economy (Rom. 5:5). The Son and the Spirit share a fellowship of love for the Father, for we must assume that in the ontological Trinity it is by the Spirit that the Son cries out "Abba, Father," just as Jesus did in the Garden (Mark 14:36) and we also do in prayer (Rom. 8:15; Gal. 4:6). The Father and the Spirit enjoy a communion of love for the Son in the ontological Trinity, just as they did when the Father poured out the love gift of the Spirit on Jesus at His baptism and, in the Spirit, announced His love for the Son: "This is My Son, the beloved, with whom I am well pleased!"[13]

The mutual indwelling of the three Persons in a perfect fellowship of love is structured, but not static, ordered—God is a God of peace, not confusion (1 Cor. 14:33)—but not mechanical. The structure of the covenant among the Persons of the Trinity is a flow, a cascade, a surge—the mutual outpouring and reception of abundant covenant life and love.

---

[12] Ibid.

[13] Ralph Allan Smith, *The Baptism of Jesus the Christ* (Eugene, OR: Wipf & Stock, 2010), 40-52.

CHAPTER 5

THE STORY OF
THE COVENANT

All who take the Bible seriously as the Word of God acknowledge that the Bible is a grand narrative: the story
of the original creation in Genesis 1-2 which finally cul-
minates in a new heavens and a new earth in the fulfillment of all in Revelation 21-22. The biblical drama
has a very clear and wonderful beginning, but the "all-
is-very-good" start of human history is interrupted by
Satan's temptation and the sin of Adam. From Genesis 3
to the end of the story, the way is complicated and various Christian groups disagree about how to interpret the
unfolding narrative. However, the connections between
the beginning and the end of the biblical story are un-
disputed, since the book of Revelation itself draws clear
attention to them. In fact, if we only read the beginning
and the end, we have to conclude that Satan's attempt to

destroy God's kingdom project was a complete failure. When we see the New Jerusalem descend from heaven to earth, we realize that during the apparently meandering path of the history from Genesis to Revelation, God was actually building the kingdom He originally planned.

Concerning the intervening story, Lutherans seem to see it as the gift of grace in a world of oppressive law—oppressive because of the sinfulness of man, not because of God's law itself. The whole Bible is about law—which condemns—and grace—which promises mercy, forgiveness, and life to condemned sinners. It seems fair to say that, in the Lutheran view, the topics of grace and law are the central concern of the story.

Reformed and Presbyterian Christians who follow "the-Covenant-of-Works-versus-the-Covenant-of-Grace" paradigm of the Westminster Confession may be more flexible in their approach to biblical history,[1] but, as I pointed out previously, the bi-covenantal scheme is a hindrance to the development of a full-fledged approach to the biblical story. In what way? This is repetition but, first, the "Covenant of Works," though not really found in the Bible, dominates the whole approach to the point that even the "Covenant of Redemption" is a "Covenant of Works." Kline, for example, can even say,

> And our additional terms, 'Creator's' and 'with Adam,' will serve to bring out the parallel-

---

[1] See Peter J. Wallace, "The Foundations of Reformed Biblical Theology: The Development of Old Testament Theology at Old Princeton, 1812–1932" in *The Westminster Theological Journal*, vol. 59, no. 1, Spring 1997.

ism between this covenant of works and what we shall be calling 'The Father's Covenant of Works with the Son' (i.e., the eternal intratrinitarian covenant), namely, the parallelism of the two Adams scheme, each of these covenants involving, as it does, an Adam figure, a federal representative under probation in a covenant of works."[2]

Kline is not by any means alone in this. Geerhardus Vos, considered one of the founding fathers of Reformed Biblical theology and an advocate of a historical approach to the Bible, also sees the "Covenant of Redemption" within the framework of the "Covenant of Works."[3]

---

[2] Meredith G. Kline, *Kingdom Prologue: Genesis Foundations for a Covenantal Worldview* (Overland Park, KS: Two Age Press, 2000), 20-21. Though Harold Fisch is not commenting on Kline or Reformed theology, his words seem apropos: "Are we not in danger of exchanging the tangible world of the Bible for a merely abstract construction, a diagram in which the storm and stress of history, its contradictoriness, as well as its hope and promise have no place? For if events in the Old Testament are 'structured,' they are 'structured' by the memory and promise of the Covenant. What we need is a type of structural analysis which shall embody the dynamics of the Covenant." Harold Fisch, "Ruth and the Structure of Covenant History" in *Vetus Testamentum* XXXII, 4 (1982), 426. Kline's view of the covenant undermines the biblical picture of covenantal history with its storm and stress and replaces it with an abstract construction.

[3] Wallace summarizes Vos in these words, "In its essence, Vos claimed, Reformed theology depends upon the three-fold covenant: that of works, that of redemption, and that of grace. Only if God covenanted with himself to redeem his people could salvation be accomplished. Only then could the covenant of works be fulfilled.

Second, the Reformed approach epitomized in its best representatives—the list is long and begins long before the nineteenth century—still fails to capture the genius of the biblical story of God's covenants with men. I will return to this later.

Dispensationalists offer a form of biblical theology that is different, but in the sense that they see a progress of revelation through distinctive periods of biblical history,[4] their approach is similar to that of Reformed Biblical theologians. However, Dispensationalism not only misses the centrality of the covenants in the development of history, but even discounts important "dispensational" changes in the history of Israel. I am referring to the immense "dispensational" changes from the era of Moses to David and from the exile to the post-exilic era, all of which Dispensationalists typically combine into a single "Mosaic" era.

Much more significantly, dispensationalism's fundamental error arises from its deepest presupposition.

Only then could the work of salvation be totally God's. 'For the Reformed, therefore, the entire ordo salutis...is bound to the mystical union with Christ. There is no gift that has not been earned by Him. Neither is there a gift that is not bestowed by Him.'" Peter J. Wallace, "The Foundations of Reformed Biblical Theology: The Development of Old Testament Theology at Old Princeton, 1812–1932" in *The Westminster Theological Journal*, vol. 59, no. 1, 65. On the one hand, Wallace's article shows how fully historical and biblical Reformed Biblical theology was. On the other hand, however, the quote above demonstrates its weakest feature.

[4] What Ryrie calls distinguishable economies in the outworking of God's purpose. Charles C. Ryrie, *Dispensationalism, Revised and Expanded* (Chicago: Moody Press, 1995), 37.

Dispensationalists claim that consistently "literal" inter-pretation of Scripture—for their system, an essential *sine qua non*—leads to a distinction between the Church and Israel that is so basic that they see two different peoples of God, an earthly people, Israel, and a heavenly people, the Church.[5] Ryrie quotes L. S. Chafer: "The dispensational-ist believes that throughout the ages God is pursuing two distinct purposes . . ."[6] Nothing could be more destruc-tive of a truly biblical theology, for they are attempting to re-separate Jew and Gentile after Christ had reconciled them into one body in Him, a body that includes all the elect from beginning to end. The biblical story ends with one holy city because Christ not only removed the curse of the Garden, but also the curse of Babel. The united and redeemed humanity is adorned as one bride for her husband (Rev. 21:2). There is no room for another.[7]

---

[5] Ibid., 33-34.

[6] Ibid., 33.

[7] More recent dispensationalists do not press the "two peoples" idea like older dispensationalists, but even Robert L. Saucy, who softens the distinction and emphasizes the equality of Jew and Gentile, can also say: "Thus the unification of Jew and gentile in the church does not rule out the possibility of *functional* distinctions between Israel and the other nations in the future . . ." In *Dispensationalism, Israel and the Church: The Search for Definition,* ed. by Craig A. Blaising and Darrell Bock (Grand Rapids, Zondervan, 1992), 155. Also, for another example, Saucy, *The Case for Progressive Dispensationalism: The Interface Between Dispensational and Non-Dispensational Theology* (Grand Rapids: Zondervan, 1993), 187: "By contrast, dispensation-alists affirm that Israel retains its Old Testament meaning as an ethnic people throughout the New Testament. Even though the believers in the church have come to share in the present messianic salvation

We may perhaps sum this up by saying that Lutherans properly understand that the biblical story is about God's grace. Reformed theologians correctly perceive the centrality of the covenantal idea. Dispensationalists rightly emphasize the progress of revelation through distinct eras in which God works in different ways. James Jordan, I believe, combines the best insights of each group, but he sees their insights in the framework of a fundamentally different kind of narrative.

Jordan, building upon his Reformed predecessors, revised them in two important ways. First, he eliminated the unbiblical "Covenant of Works"—though in that he was not unique, as he himself points out.[8]

Second, the key to the unfolding history of God's covenants with man—the *genius* of the biblical story of God's covenants with men—is the fact that God was bringing His people to maturity, ultimately to eternal union between God and man in His covenant love and grace. Jordan outlines the history of biblical covenants

---

along with Jews and the church is now serving God's kingdom purpose, Israel in its historic meaning will yet fulfill its promised destiny." Similarly, the more recent, Michael Vlach, *Dispensationalism: Essential Beliefs and Common Myths: Revised and Updated* (Colorado Springs, CO: Theological Studies Press, 2017). Even in the progressive view, the body of Christ is not one, but two.

[8] James B. Jordan, "Merit Versus Maturity: What Did Jesus Do for Us?" in Steve Wilkins and Duane Garner, ed. *The Federal Vision* (Monroe, LA: Athanasius Press, 2004). This is not to deny that Jesus was commissioned with a special work and that He fulfilled it to the joy of His Father. But that does not imply that the eternal Son was or could have been "on probation" in any meaningful sense of the expression.

from the first Adam to the last as a succession of covenants in which each covenant exhibits growth and development from the previous. These covenants are not presented as "contracts" or "agreements" but documented expressions of an ongoing relationship between God and the sons to whom He grants His covenant—a movement, however labyrinthine, from childhood to maturity.

As Jordan expounds the story—again not uniquely —there is a succession of covenants.[9] In the Old Covenant era, there are covenants with Adam (priestly), Noah (kingly), Abraham (prophetic), Moses (priestly), David (kingly), and the exiles returned to Judah (prophetic). The New Covenant in Christ (ultimate and final Priest, King and Prophet) fulfills the whole meaning of the covenantal history before Him. From Adam until Jesus, the covenant history is revelation in shadow form. In Jesus, the light of God's truth shines brightly.

Why is this important? It means that God's work in history is not merely or even primarily "repair." Satan did not win in the Garden. There is, no doubt, a tragic element in the history of biblical covenants. For every covenant in the old era—the era of the first Adam—ends in sin and judgment, like Adam in the Garden. But where sin abounded, grace did much more abound, for every judgment leads to a new and more glorious covenant. The progress of God's work in history is not overthrown either by Satan or by human sin. We can almost say that it is hardly hindered. The biblical drama of God's historical

---

[9] My presentation here is quite simplified. For a fuller discussion, see, Jordan, *Through New Eyes*, 167-289.

covenants is the story of God—He is the main character—building the kingdom He always intended to build,
in spite of Satan's opposition and man's sin and failure.

To put this in different words, the biblical story of
the covenant is partially tragic while being fundamentally and finally comic. The story of the covenants that
God has given to men is tragic in the sense that every
covenant era of the old covenant age, from Adam to the
new covenant in Christ, ended in failure and judgment.
Adam was expelled from the Garden, but he named Eve
as a confession of his faith in God's promise (Gen. 3:20).
He had hope for the future. However, in the generations
after him, the sinfulness of mankind spread so compre-
hensively that God brought the judgment of the flood
on the whole world. The first era ended in the tragedy
of worldwide sin and death—the sin in the Garden and
the judgment of expulsion magnified almost beyond all
bounds, virtually erasing the history from Genesis 1:2
until the flood.

But that is not the end of the story—as we will see in
a later chapter—nor is it the essence of the story. Grace
followed judgement, grace that exalted Noah and his descendants to a higher level of covenantal responsibility
and a higher level of revelation. Then, in the tower of
Babel rebellion, Nimrod and the descendants of Noah
repeated Adam's fall and the apostasy of the whole race
before the flood. Grace is followed by tragedy, but again
the story does not end in tragedy. Babelic tragedy is followed by greater grace, for God chose Abraham to be a
new channel of blessing to all mankind. Genesis ends on
a note of hope, with Abraham's seed at the right hand of

power bringing salvation to Israel and the world. To repeat: man's sin and folly cannot overwhelm the ongoing progress of God's gracious kingdom[10] because the kingdom eschatology was set from the beginning.

As with Eden and Babel, the story of grace—followed by betrayal and sin resulting in judgment—repeats itself in the subsequent covenant eras of Moses, David, and after the exile. But whenever sin seemed to infect and ruin everything, the power of grace brought healing and blessing. Still, until Jesus came as the last Adam to create in Himself a new human race, mankind lived and moved "in Adam," imitating his rebellion and provoking judgment. But we misread the story if we see a mere cycle of sin, failure, and judgment.

Even in the old era, biblical history is the story of God's covenantal grace, not only forgiving sin, but also

---

[10] Leithart's description of the progress of grace in the gift of the tabernacle is noteworthy: "Yahweh drove Adam and Eve out of the garden; he invited Aaron and his sons in. For the first time since Eden, a human being stood before the Creator to serve. Not Noah, not Abraham, not Jacob or Joseph: none of them passed by the cherubim to take up the Adamic task to stand and serve within Yahweh's garden. For the first time since Yahweh stationed cherubim at the gate of the garden, Torah allowed human beings to take over the Adamic task to "guard" the garden (šāmar, Gen 2:15). For the first time since Adam, holy men walked on holy ground, with only a veil embroidered with cherubim between them and Yahweh. The tabernacle was still holy space, but the boundaries of holy space had become porous. Yahweh expelled Adam from the garden in wrath, and put Adam under wrath. In the tabernacle system, Yahweh went out into the howling waste to find his unfaithful bride and bring her back home. He went outside Eden to give a taste of Eden to Adam's children who lived east of Eden." *Delivered from the Elements*, 95.

bringing mankind to maturity. With the coming of the Second Adam and the inauguration of the New Covenant, the Holy Spirit is poured out on Christ's body, the church, to empower her to growth. Jesus' Great Commission was a command to the Church for world conquest: "Disciple the nations!"

The Bible provides a framework within which to view this progression of covenants including its "storm and stress:" death and resurrection. Because of the sin of Adam, death became a curse and an enemy. But it was not so originally. In the plant world, for example, the principle of death and resurrection preceded the fall: ". . .unless a grain of wheat falls into the ground and dies, it remains alone; but if it dies, it produces much grain" (John 12:24). That was no less true in the Garden than any time after the fall. Death, in other words, is not necessarily curse.

Thus, even for mankind before the fall, there is what Jordan calls "good death." What does that mean? Jordan explains that Adam's "deep sleep" in Genesis 2:21 is something much more than "sleep." The Hebrew word הַמַּרְדֵּת (tardemah) is "associated with de-creation or death, especially in covenant-making acts of God." Again, "Deep-sleep is close to death and is the place where covenants are made; it is de-creation preceding either total death or resurrection."[11]

---

[11] James B. Jordan, *From Bread to Wine: Creation, Worship, and Christian Maturity,* 86. Athanasius Press. Kindle Edition. Jordan expounds this concept through many examples. The relevant Hebrew words occur in the following passages, most of which Jordan touches on: Genesis 2:21; 15:12; Judges 4:21; 1 Samuel 26:12; Job 4:13; 33:15;

This is seen in the creation of the woman:

> Adam goes into deep-sleep and "dies" to his
> state of being alone. Then, from his side, God
> makes a partner for him. When Adam awakes,
> he is in covenant union with his wife. This cov-
> enant is made through blood, for it is not just
> a rib but a whole flesh-and-bone (and blood)
> piece of Adam that is made into Eve; as Adam
> says, "This is flesh of my flesh, bone of my
> bone." And Adam also says that man must "die"
> to his old family to make a new one: "For this
> cause a man shall leave his father and mother
> and cleave to his wife."[12]

The principle of death and resurrection, then, is not limited to the post-fall situation. It is fundamental to the way that God created the world and to the whole process of growth and development. In other words, in the Bible's depiction of a series of covenants, we really have a story, a narrative of growth and development culminating in an everlasting resurrection that reveals the meaning and direction of the whole of history from Eden to New Jerusalem.

Every covenant era in the time from Adam to Christ ended in death because of sin: the whole world was "in

---

Psalms 76:6; Proverbs 10:5; 19:15; Isaiah 29:10; Daniel 8:18; 10:9; Jonah 1:5–6. Note, the Hebrew word רדם is derived from the noun הַמְדַּרֵת.

[12] Ibid., 88.

Adam." But after each death, God graciously resurrected His people and brought the world into a more glorious covenant than the previous one. However, something more was needed: a new Adam that would not repeat Adam's fall, a new Adam that could father a whole new race. Only the incarnation of God Himself could accomplish that.

One reason that Jesus came into the world as a new Adam was to take away the curse that the first Adam brought upon the whole race. But to do that, He first had to be a new Israel. He had to fulfill the story that began with God's choice of Abraham to be the one through whom both the curse of Eden and the curse of Babel would be overcome.

Thus, Leithart explains:

> By his death as a penal substitute, Jesus demolished the old order and inaugurated a new world. Jesus was a penal substitute for the world because he was first of all a penal substitute *for Israel,* because he ransomed Israel from the curse and constituted a new Israel to live by the *nomos* of the Spirit and to be sent on a mission to call the nations to share that culture. He was a penal substitute for the sins of the world insofar as he made a way of forgiveness and reconciliation with God through the new Israel.
>
> Jesus was not only the true Israel and the world's king but also the Last Adam, the "Son of Man" who has come to tame the bestial empires that rise from the turbulent sea (Dan 7).

This is something of an extrapolation from the gospel story, but it seems a legitimate one: Jews and Gentiles, which for the Bible constitute the sum of the human race, executed the Son of Man for the crimes they themselves committed. *They* punished him for their sins, and so made him their penal substitute for the sins of humanity.[13]

Jesus came as the True Israel to fulfill all that Israel had been called to do and take upon Himself the covenant curse she deserved and in so doing take upon Himself the curses that all mankind deserved. Gentiles and Jews together condemned and crucified the Son of Man. But God vindicated Him by raising Him from the dead. The resurrected Jesus brought new life in a truly new covenant, one that did not merely introduce another era of failure and judgment. Moreover, Jesus was not simply alive, rather than dead. His resurrection body was a new kind of body, one that could not die. In this new body, He ascended into heaven and sat down at the right hand of God. The good news is that all authority in heaven and on earth has been granted to Him. Therefore, on Pentecost He could pour out the Holy Spirit and begin the formation of His body, the church: a new humanity with a new covenant Head.

We see, then, that the repeated deaths and resurrections of distinct covenant eras within the larger Adamic era all pointed forward to the death and resurrection of

---

[13] Leithart, *Delivered from the Elements*, 164-65.

the last Adam. Every death and resurrection is a type of the death and resurrection of the Seed to come. The biblical history of the world is typological and it is all fulfilled in Jesus, or rather, it is all fulfilled in the story of Jesus and His bride, the church, for it was not good for Him to be alone. From the time of His ascension, He is building His church by the work of the Spirit until all is fulfilled in the descent of the New Jerusalem to earth as the eternal abode of the Lamb and His bride.

Erich Auerbach—a secular Jew living during the Nazi era as an exile in Istanbul—saw this typological aspect of biblical history, as Edward Said in the introduction to *Mimesis* explains.

> Basically, figural interpretation develops as early Christian thinkers such as Tertullian and Augustine felt impelled to reconcile the Old with the New Testament. Both parts of the Bible were the word of God, but how were they related, how could they be read, as it were, together, given the quite considerable difference between the old Judaic dispensation and the new message emanating from the Christian Incarnation?
>
> The solution arrived at, according to Auerbach, is the notion that the Old Testament prophetically prefigures the New Testament, which in turn can be read as a figural and, he adds, carnal (hence incarnate, real, worldly) realization or interpretation of the Old Testament. The first event or figure is "real and historical announcing something else that is also real and

historical" (*Drama of European Literature,* 29). At last we begin to see, like interpretation itself, how history does not only move forward but also backward, in each oscillation between eras managing to accomplish a greater realism, a more substantial "thickness" (to use a term from current anthropological description), a higher degree of truth.[14]

Only Jordan's typological approach to the biblical narrative, from its seed in Genesis 1-2 to the full fruit in Revelation 21-22, does justice to the story from the beginning to the end. Yes, there is law and grace and there are distinct periods in God's management of the world. Certainly covenant is a central theme. But unless we see the story as a succession of deaths that God in His grace brings to resurrection in a new and better world—which was His original plan from the beginning—we do not really have a "story" at all. Unless we see that the whole history of the world typologically points to Jesus Himself

---

[14] Erich Auerbach, *Mimesis: The Representation of Reality in Western Literature* (Princeton, NJ: Princeton University Press, Fiftieth-Anniversary Edition 2003), xiii. Auerbach's original and quite technical essay, "Figura" appears in *Selected Essays of Erich Uerbach: Time, History, and Literature,* ed. by James I. Porter (Princeton: Princeton University Press, 2014). The point of referring to Auerbach is to show that the typological nature of the biblical story is obvious even to a secular Jew, because he knows literary history and is sensitive to literary forms and expressions. Jordan's emphasis on typology is characteristically Christian. Bringing up new themes is just building on the past.

and the ultimate salvation of His bride, there is no united and meaningful story.

This, however, raises another question: in all of this, does the economy of God's work in the history of the covenants somehow reveal Trinitarian ontology? We may answer the question with a question: If there were nothing analogous in the ontology of the Triune God, how would the death and resurrection of the Son of God be possible?

Leithart, arguing against Derrida—who can only imagine a son who is in some way a "depletion" of his father—asserts the full equality of Father, Son, and Spirit, but also adds:

> We may even speak of self-giving (death) and return (resurrection) in the life of God. The Father loves and submits to the Son, and the Son to the Father, and Son to the Spirit, and so on and on. But this self-giving of one Person to the others is always met with a return gift: The Father's gift of himself to the Son is met with the Son's gift of himself to the Father. Their "self-sacrifice" is met with renewed fellowship. Death and resurrection, of course, is *the* comic theme, and there is thus a 'comic' structure to the Triune life, an eternal "story" of "emanation and remanation," of exile and return. Because this is the God who created and governs history, history manifests the same structure, and it is a story not of a golden age lost, nor even of a return to Edenic paradise, but a story

in which the second moment, the final moment, is the glory of the first.[15]

The biblical story of the covenants as a story of death and resurrection reflects the ontology of the Father, Son, and Spirit—the covenant life of the Triune God—because each Person of the Trinity delights to deny Himself for the glory of the other. The incarnation and death and resurrection of Jesus manifest this clearly. Jesus did not regard His own glory as most important, but considered His people more important than Himself, so He willingly went to the cross (Phil. 2:3 ff.). The Father delighted in the Son's obedience and highly exalted Him in glory, so that all will bow the knee to the Son, to the glory of the Father (Phil. 2:9-11). The Father glorified the Son in the Spirit and the Son's glorification in turn glorifies the Father. In Jesus' words: "Father, the hour has come. Glorify Your Son, that Your Son also may glorify You" (John 17:1).

In the story of covenant history after the fall, death is the wages of sin. Thus, tragedy in the biblical story is genuine—contrary to the assertions of Karl Jaspers[16]—and the terrifying consequences of rebellion against God may be eternal. But the Triune God of covenant life does not allow death-as-wages-for-sin to have the last word.

---

[15] Peter J. Leithart, "Supplement at the Origin: Trinity, Eschatology and History" in *International Journal of Systematic Theology*, vol. 6, no. 4, October 2004, 385-86.

[16] Jaspers insisted that "no genuinely Christian tragedy can exist." Karl Jaspers, *Tragedy is Not Enough,* trans. Harold A. T. Reiche, Harry T. Moore, and Karl W. Deutsch (Boston: Beacon Press, 1953), 38.

The conclusion to the Bible story is "comic," ending as it does in the resurrection of a new humanity as the Bride of Christ with the New Jerusalem united with God in an everlasting fulness of life and love. With respect to the Trinity, the story of the covenant as death and resurrection points to the fellowship of the Trinity as fellowship in self-denial and glorification of the other, a mutual self-denial and glorification that flows as an endless river of life.

CHAPTER 6

THE CEREMONIES
OF THE COVENANT

Someone reading the Bible for the first time might conclude, especially after perusing Exodus and Leviticus, that the biblical God loves ceremonies. That naive impression would not actually be wrong, for the creation of the world itself as recorded in Genesis 1-2 is basically ceremonial—a covenant-making rite. God's method of instructing Adam and his wife by means of trees in the midst of the Garden was ceremonial: it was not by looking at the trees or meditating on their names that Adam would understand. God talked about eating. When Adam took and ate, the world suddenly changed.

After the fall, God instituted animal sacrifice, clothing Adam and his newly named wife (Gen. 3:20) in animal skins to cover the nakedness the fall exposed. Cain and Abel both knew that God required the sacrifice of an animal—shed blood to cover sin—but Cain rebelled. After Cain and Abel, faithful men like Noah and Abraham offer bloody ascension offerings[1] to worship the true God.

The animal sacrifices and laws about clean and unclean—already known by Noah (Gen. 8:20)—were part of a pedagogy of "elementary principles," a pedagogy that was greatly expanded and elaborated with the full gift of the Torah and its laws and sacrifices. The sign of circumcision, given to Abraham, initiated a new era in what Leithart calls "Yahweh's war against the flesh." What does he mean by "flesh"[2] and why would Yahweh be at war with it?

The use of the word "flesh" in the Bible is complex. Perhaps most Christians will think first of the apostle Paul's use when he contrasts the works of the flesh with the fruit of the Spirit (Gal. 5:19-26). But when God created Adam, Adam was "flesh" and so was the woman

---

[1] The usual translation is "whole burnt offering," but the Hebrew is just "go up offering," which is best rendered as "ascension offering." The sacrificed animal ascends to God in the place of the offerer who cannot approach God because of his sins. The only way back into the Garden is through the Door of Death. Fallen man cannot approach God directly, so he must offer a substitute to die in his place and ascend in smoke. The so-called "whole burnt offering" is not about burning whole, but about approaching the God who expelled Adam from Eden, the God who can only be approached through the Door of Death.

[2] Leithart devotes an entire chapter to the discussion of the concept of flesh in his *Delivered from the Elements of the World: Atonement, Justification, Mission*, 75-90. My PDF software tells me that the word "flesh" appears over one thousand times in Leithart's book!

who was created from him: "flesh of my flesh." In the creation story, "flesh" does not connote "sinful lust." On the contrary, "Adam and Eve were created as flesh—limited, weak, vulnerable, touchable, woundable. That was good, *very* good."[3] All that Adam and Eve had to do was rely on their heavenly Father, believing His Word and resting in His gracious care. Though they were naked and immature, they had nothing to fear from the fact of their weakness.

But Adam gave in to Satan's temptation and rebelled against God. When God cast Adam and Eve out of the Garden, they had suffered a profound transformation:

> Outside Eden, Adam and Eve were still flesh, but something had changed. Adam and his children were not only weak and dependent but also now delivered over to the reign of Death and Sin, in corruptible, shameful and now *mortal* flesh. . . . Because of Adam's sin, death came to all. According to Paul, death came into the world on the heels of sin, so that after Adam death spread to all people (Rom 5). And when death spreads, sin spreads.[4]

Leithart explains: "Drawing on the Old Testament, Paul uses 'flesh' as a 'master metaphor' to describe the condition of humanity following the fall."[5] After the fall, flesh

---

[3] Ibid., 75.

[4] Ibid., 76-77.

[5] Ibid., 78.

comes to have meanings associated with sin, pride, and rebellion, so—to answer the question above—God took up
a war against the flesh. Animal sacrifice and distinctions
between clean and unclean were part of that warfare.

In the Genesis story, the judgment of the flood was
total warfare against the flesh on a global scale. When
Noah's descendants, led by Nimrod, renewed human
rebellion against God, God's judgment of the flesh was
gracious. However, the judgement of the tower of Babel
introduced deep divisions into "fleshly" humanity, which
the call of Abraham was intended to eventually heal.

The story of Abraham, however, is odd. It is written so that the reader will be perplexed, asking what God
is doing and why. Consider: at the age of seventy-five,
childless Abram is given a promise from God that he
would become a great nation and that through him all
the nations of the earth would be blessed—thus undoing
both the curse from Eden and from Babel. But for many
long years, the promise is not fulfilled. Finally, when he is
ninety-nine years old, God appears to Abram again and
renews the promise in fuller terms: Abram will be the father of a multitude of nations, including many kings and
a seed so abundant, he needs to have his name changed
to "Abraham" to make the promise clear (Gen. 17:1-14).
With the overwhelming emphasis of the covenant seed
given to a man with no covenant child, God also gives a
covenant sign. Cut off your flesh! Circumcision is symbolic castration: the ultimate confession of one's inability
to be a father. From that time onward, every child in the
line of Abraham is circumcised when eight days old, not
at ninety-nine years of age. But they all know and repeat-

edly hear the story of Abraham. If they listen rightly, they know that God is telling them that they do not have what it takes to bear the promised seed. The promised seed must come from God, not from "flesh." And one year later, now that Abraham was good and dead, the promised seed is born, with laughter (Gen. 17:19, 21; 21:1-7; Isaac means "laugh," and Sarah confessed that God made her laugh; Gen. 21:6).

The story of Abraham is the opposite of the story of Adam. Adam could not wait for the promise to be fulfilled and so he took from the temporarily forbidden tree. Though Abraham had his moments of impatience, he did wait and follow. His patient faith was rewarded with a child whose name reminded him daily of the grace of God until the day that God said to him, "Take now your son, your only son Isaac, whom you love, and go to the land of Moriah, and offer him there as an ascension offering on one of the mountains of which I shall tell you" (Gen. 22:2). Abraham, the New Testament tells us, trusted God so fully that he knew that even if he offered Isaac up as a sacrifice, God would raise him from the dead to fulfill his promise—which in a manner of speaking He did (Heb. 11:19).

Isaac was born from a castrated father and a dead mother and was himself killed as a sacrifice: the covenant given to Abraham was indeed God's war against Adamic flesh. Laughter had to come from the special working of God's grace and it did.

The covenant given to Israel at Sinai took the war against the flesh to a new and higher level. Now that the seed of Abraham had become a nation, the war against the flesh had to be incorporated into every aspect of the national life in the land that God promised to Abraham. The Exodus itself was Yahweh's destruction of the Satanic Pharaoh, the man who sang the song of fleshly boasting: "I will pursue, I will overtake, I will divide the spoil; My desire shall be satisfied on them. I will draw my sword, My hand shall destroy them" (Exod. 15:9).[6]

The firstborn of Egypt died, but the firstborn of all Israel survived by the death of the lamb. When Yahweh gave them a tabernacle, priests, and a sacrificial system, the war against the flesh was waged in full ceremonial splendor. Laws of clean and unclean, laws about food, laws about crimes and daily life in the land—in short, everything in the laws from Exodus to Deuteronomy— were all part of Yahweh's war against the flesh. The whole Torah was an anti-flesh pedagogy preparing the way for the Messiah: the incarnate Son of God who would take upon Himself human flesh—tabernacle among us (John 1:14)—in order to die for the sons of Adam and offer resurrection life to those who believe.[7]

Jordan works out this ceremonial history from a somewhat different but complementary perspective.

> Patterns of historical movement are of tremen-
> dous importance in the Bible. These sequenc-

---

[6] Handel's *Israel in Egypt* perfectly captures the irony of Pharaoh's vain boast and Yahweh's judgment.

[7] The paragraphs above represent a grossly oversimplified summary of one aspect of Leithart's book, *Delivered from the Elements of the World.*

es correspond, in various ways, to the order of the sacrifices, the sequence of the sacrifices, the ritual of covenant renewal, the biographies of individuals, and the course of human history. This series of essays reflects on aspects of some of the fundamental ways this basic contour of history is set forth in the Bible and how it is encapsulated in biblical rituals. In short, what I am seeking to develop is a unified theological understanding of history, biography, and ritual. The fundamental thesis that underlies these studies is that biblical rituals are not something strange or different from the pattern of human life, but that those rituals move through the same steps as human life and thus are designed to key us in to God's ways, His paths in this world. Sin has distorted the rhythm of human life, but the rituals in the Bible help restore our rhythm by duplicating human life in a small, short, compact, and stylized way. Just as the Tabernacle is a small, or microcosmic, replica of the whole cosmos, so biblical rituals are short, or microchronic, replicas of (macrochronic) human history and of human biography. Comparing biblical rituals with biblical history and biblical biographies should provide us with a better vision of how we can live our lives under God's guiding hand.[8]

---

[8] Jordan, James B.. *From Bread to Wine: Creation, Worship, and Christian Maturity*, 6. Athanasius Press. Kindle Edition.

Biblical rituals offer patterns for us to re-shape our lives so that we can bear fruit for God's kingdom!

By contrast to the rather complex and elaborate Mosaic economy, in the new covenant, there are only two rituals and they are both relatively simple: baptism and the Lord's Supper. There is no New Testament instruction about the ritual of baptism itself: Which day of the week? How old must the child be? Must it be public? Sprinkle, pour, dunk? etc. Jesus commanded us to baptize "into the Name of the Father and of the Son and of the Holy Spirit" (Matt. 28:19), distinctly covenantal language. Beyond that, there is no detailed direction about baptism. What we have are examples in the books of Acts, examples that suggest that the day of the week and the time of day, the place, and all the rest are irrelevant. Also, it is important to note that in the Bible, baptism is never part of a worship service. Baptism is not an aspect of Christian worship; it is the prerequisite for Christian worship.

The other new covenant ritual is the Lord's Supper. It was clearly a part of the weekly worship of the early church (1 Cor. 11:20-21, 23ff.), though that is not specifically commanded, and there is no detailed instruction about the performance of the ritual that is set down for all churches in all places to perform at all times. If we ask why the new covenant does not include the kind of ritual specifics that the Mosaic Torah did, the answer is at least twofold. First, Israel was a nation in the childhood era of God's covenantal leading (Gal. 3:23-25; 4:1-3), so Yahweh instructed His child about what to wear, what to eat, where to live, and gave His child a calendar for the year—actually for seven even-year cycles culminating in a fiftieth year Jubilee—with detailed instructions about festivals and sacrifices. Now that we are sons, God expects us to learn from the example of His instruction to Israel and then to formulate our own ways in submission to Him. Second, unlike ancient Israel, the church does not have a special land given by God—or, rather, God has given the whole earth to the church, but the Gospel conquest takes time. The church as an international, multi-linguistic, multiracial body must adjust to the circumstances she faces in various localities and cultures according to the maturity of the church at the time.[9]

But the church can and should learn from old covenant ritual and, as circumstances allow, apply that to her own worship. What might churches learn from old covenant ritual that could apply to their worship in new covenant circumstances? To answer this, we must first note that worship in the new covenant is patterned after the tabernacle/temple worship (Rom. 12:1; Heb. 13:15; etc.) and therefore we must recollect the basics of Mosaic worship and the offering of sacrifice.

The sacrificial animal in Mosaic worship is offered to God in three steps: 1) the animal is slaughtered and its blood splashed on the altar; 2) the animal is skinned and cut up for offering; 3) the animal is burned, transformed

---

[9] Thus, for example, almost all Christians agree that Sunday morning is the ideal time for Christian worship because Christ arose from the dead on Sunday morning, but the New Testament does not command Christians to worship on Sunday morning and there may be times and places, especially when the church is being persecuted, that Sunday morning worship is not possible.

into smoke to ascend to Yahweh.[10] There were also three main types of sacrifice: 1) the purification offering; 2) the ascension offering; 3) the peace offering.[11] As Meyers explains, these sacrifices were always offered in this order. The significance is that the purification offering brought cleansing and forgiveness, after which the worshipper can ascend into God's presence through the animal who represents him. Then, the worshipper can enjoy a fellowship meal with God, for in the peace offering there is a portion for Yahweh, a portion for the priest, and a portion for the worshipper. The aim and meaning of the Mosaic sacrificial ritual was covenant renewal.

Mosaic sacrificial ritual thus provides a pattern for worship that is easily applied to new covenant worship. We renew our covenant with the Father, Son, and Spirit according to a pattern that can be outlined in five steps: 1) the call to worship, corresponding to the priests blowing the trumpets to assemble the people; 2) confession of sin and cleansing, corresponding to the purification offering; 3) ascension to God to pray and hear His word, cor-

---

[10] Jeffrey J. Meyers, *The Lord's Service: The Grace of Covenant Renewal Worship* (Moscow, ID: Canon Press, 2003), 78-79.

[11] Ibid., 80. The "purification offering" is usually called "sin offering" in Bible translations and the "ascension offering" is usually called the "whole burnt offering." As I pointed out above, the naming of the "whole burnt offering" is especially misleading, for the Hebrew just means "go up." In his introduction to Leviticus, Everett Fox writes, "The first chapter begins with a description of the *ola*, the "offering up . . ." *The Five Books of Moses: The Schocken Bible, Volume I*, translated by Everett Fox (New York: Schoken Books, 1995), 510. "Ascension" is a literal translation of the Hebrew that clearly shows the significance of the offering, drawing near to God.

responding to the ascension offering; 4) fellowship with God in the Lord's Supper, corresponding to the peace offering; 5) dismissal with blessing, corresponding to the Levitical blessing in Numbers 6:24-26.[12]

What is important for this essay, however, is what Jordan has detailed extensively in various writings—not only in *From Bread to Wine*—that God created us as ritual beings. Ritual and ceremony are in our bones—perhaps I should say, in our DNA!—because we are created as the image of God. As God's image, we cannot escape being "ceremonial." Thus, we see clearly that rejecting God does not "liberate" men from their ritual nature. Note the excessive—and sometimes ludicrous—rituals and ceremonies of atheist nations: Soviet Russia, Communist China, North Korea, etc. Men cannot live without ceremonies because we are created in the image of a God who loves ceremonies and ritual. We are created as the image of a ceremonial God!

If the economy reflects the ontology and the economy is, by God's design, full of ritual, what is the ritual in God? What is His ceremony?

We return here to eternal generation and eternal spiration.[13] The Father's eternal generation of the Son is essential to His being the Father, even as being generated is

---

[12] There is much more that needs to be said about this. For a full explanation and justification of this pattern, see Meyers, op. cit.

[13] To speak more fully, Bavinck refers to: "the so-called 'personal properties': (1) paternity ('unbegottenness,' active generation, and active spiration); (2) filiation or sonship, passive generation, active spiration; (3) procession or passive spiration." Herman Bavinck, *Reformed Dogmatics, Volume 2: God and Creation*.

essential to the Son being the Son. The Spirit as the agent
of generation and the breathed out love from Father to
Son and back to Father again is no less essential to the
Triune being of God. This is to say that eternal generation
and spiration are necessary acts of God. The Father, Son,
and Spirit live a life of eternal generation and spiration
because God cannot be other than He essentially is. His
existence is necessary existence as Father, Son, and Spirit.
Thus, the Triune God exists necessarily as a God in whom
the ritual of generation and spiration constitutes His very
Triune Being. Why do I use the word "ritual"? Because
generation and spiration are words that describe a "movement" of a sort, a dance of life. The Father generates the
Son, and together with the Son spirates the Spirit in an
overflowing and eternal ceremony of mutual glorification—giving and sharing.

Though he is not speaking of the Triune God as a
ritual God, the necessity of the relations is well expressed
in Emery's account of Aquinas' thought:

> What Thomas is rejecting is the idea that the
> person who exercises an action can be conceived
> extra-relationally, independently of his consti-
> tution as person through his relative property.
> Otherwise put, the role of relations is not re-
> stricted to putting the persons on show. The rel-
> ative properties are not adventitiously added on
> to persons who have already been constituted in
> some other way. We can express it as St Albert
> does: one cannot think a distinct person other
> than by grasping his relative property. Since the

actions are not performed by the divine essence but rather by the persons as such (it is the person of the Father which engenders), the Father cannot be grasped as an acting subject outside his relative property of paternity. This is why, in the order of our understanding of the mystery, getting hold of paternity, the property of the Father, comes before grasping the personal action performed by the Father. Otherwise, one would have conceive[d] the Father independently of his relative property or anteriorly to this relative property. Attached to his doctrine of relation, St Thomas shows that this is not possible, because it boils down to conceiving the Father in some way as a pre-relational divine being. He does not conceive the Father as the "absolute person of God" but rather conceives the one who is the Father through his paternity.[14]

For the same reason, if we prescind from the relations which are the three personal properties (paternity, filiation, procession), then the divine persons evaporate from our thought.... If we abstract from the relations, then within our minds at least, the tri-personhood of God vanishes. Without the relative properties of paternity, filiation, and procession, it becomes impossible to conceive the divine persons,

---

[14] Gilles Emery, *The Trinitarian Thought of Thomas Aquinas* (Oxford: Oxford University Press, 2007), 125-26.

since it is these relative properties which distinguish and constitute the persons. The reason which Thomas gives for this goes back to one of Albert's formulae. There is not, on the one hand, person, and on the other hand, relation, but "the relations bear their supposits within themselves."[15]

Relations are necessary for they constitute the Persons, but the relations are not "mechanical." Thus, at the same time that we affirm their necessity, we must also say that the Father's generation of the Son, as well as the Father and the Son's "breathing out" the Spirit are voluntary acts, for these are expressions of intra-trinitarian love, and the love of God must be and is eternally free.

That the intra-trinitarian life of God must be both necessary and free is not a contradiction. God is who He is necessarily because He cannot be other than He eternally is. But freedom and love are no less necessary to His being than existence itself, for He is never naked "being." The Father must be Father as the One who generates the Son, but that existential necessity is not a rule "outside the Father" by which the Father is bound. He generates the Son in the freedom of His absolute love for the Son. The same freedom and love characterizes all that we can say of the Son and the Spirit. Generation and spiration are necessary, but nevertheless free, because the Triune God is necessarily free and loving, a mystery that we cannot fathom, but which we can enjoy and give thanks for.

---

[15] Ibid., 126.

This account of eternal generation is somewhat different from that of Jonathan Edwards as Larson represents him.[16] In Edwards' view, the eternal generation of the Son is an act of God glorifying Himself through the perfect idea of Himself. Though there is some truth in this, I think it may be misleading. We should rather say that the Father's act of generating the Son is an act of glorifying an "Other." In generating the Son, the Father shares His own glory with the Son, for He generates the Son as the radiance of His glory (Heb. 1:3). The Father glorifies the Son in the very act of generation and the Son in filiation glorifies the Father in the Spirit of glory who proceeds from the Father and the Son. Mutual glorification depicts the ritual reality of the Trinity.

The assertions above are, of course, grounded in the economy. The Son, who in His incarnate ministry spoke of Himself as seeking the glory of the One who sent Him (John 7:18), did as the God-man what He had done eternally before the incarnation: He sought the glory of the Father He loved, for He responded to the Father by glorifying the One who had glorified Him. Similarly,

---

[16] Christina N. Larson, "Jonathan Edwards and Eternal Generation," *Retrieving Eternal Generation,* ed. by Fred Sanders and Scott Swain (Grand Rapids: Zondervan, 2017). "In *nuce*, Edwards first reckons that if God is infinitely happy in himself, God must have self-understanding or an idea of himself as the object of his delight: 'the sum of his inclination, love and joy is his love to and delight in himself' because 'the sum of the divine understanding and wisdom consists in his having a perfect idea of himself.' For Edwards, the divine happiness is free—entirely independent of causes external to the divine life—because the eternal divine idea is the perfect image of the divine glory."

Jesus told His disciples that the Spirit of Truth would guide them into all Truth and glorify the Son, with the implication that the Father is also glorified thereby (John 16:13-15). The fellowship of mutual glorification that we see in the economy points to an eternal fellowship of mutual glorification grounded in eternal generation and eternal spiration.

In different words, the Triune God Himself is an eternal ceremony of overflowing and ever reciprocating love and life, a God in whom delight in an "Other," rejoicing in and glorifying an "Other," is essential to who He is. In glorifying the Son, the Father is not merely rejoicing in the image of Himself. He is finding supreme bliss in One who is truly and profoundly "Other," while nevertheless being wholly like Himself. The Son is more "Other" from the Father than we can imagine, while at the same time being wholly One with Him.

What the Father bestows in generating the Son is nothing other than Himself—just as also Father and Son give themselves in, through, and to the Spirit. We know that in the economy, for God to love means that He gives His Son to and for the world. Therefore, in the eternal fellowship of the Triune Persons, love is utter self-giving, nothing held back. In giving His covenant to us, God gives Himself. He is the essence of the gift of covenant love in the economy because that is who He was, is and always will be in the intra-trinitarian covenantal life.

In creating a world that manifests the glory of this sort of Triune God, God is not acting out of character; He is showing us what kind of God He is. The rhythms of the creation, the movements of the stars, sun, and moon, the seasons of the year and the life cycles of plants and animals all reflect the glory of God and the ritual reality of His Triune life. Therefore, when God created us as His image, He created us within a seven-day covenantal ceremony to reflect His own ritual reality!

CHAPTER 7

THE GOAL OF
THE COVENANT

As we have seen, God's covenantal relationship with the world began at creation, climaxing in the creation of His image, man: "So God created man in His image; in the image of God He created him; male and female He created them" (Gen. 1:27). By showing us a gradual creation over a period of six days, the creation narrative itself implies a God who works with creation to guide it from glory to glory and on the last day created man as His image to imitate His ways. Thus, having created man, God commissioned him: "Then God blessed them, and God said to them, 'Be fruitful and multiply; fill the earth and subdue it; have dominion over the fish of the sea, over the birds of the air, and over every living thing that moves on the earth'" (Gen. 1:28).

At least four things should be noted about this.[1] One, the mandate is a "blessing," distinctly covenantal language to designate a covenantal commission which is itself an honor that is given to mankind for joy and good. Two, the commission reveals God's plan and intention in creating the first pair—which means the commission reveals a biblical eschatology, for it shows where God will lead history, already suggesting a climax and fulfillment of man's historical mission. Three, though God created only one man and one woman, He planned to fill the world with His image through what we would call the "natural process" of child-bearing. Untold millions of "images" filling the world is part of the goal of history declared from the beginning. Four, God called upon man to have "dominion" over the earth. The Hebrew word for "dominion" is often used in martial contexts,[2] but there

---

[1] For a detailed exposition of this section of Genesis, Wenham is helpful: Gordon J. Wenham, *Genesis 1-15,* Word Biblical Commentary, vol. 1, (Grand Rapids: Zondervan, 1987), 26ff. For a fuller explanation of the creation story itself, including its eschatological implications, see the numerous works by James B. Jordan, who devotes attention to the creation story from various perspectives: *Through New Eyes: Developing a Biblical View of the World* (Brentwood, TN: Wolgemuth & Hyatt, Publishers, Inc., 1988), *Creation in Six Days: A Defense of the Traditional Reading of Genesis One* (Moscow, ID: Canon Press, 1999), *From Bread to Wine: Creation, Worship, and Christian Maturity* (West Monroe, LA: Athanasius Press, 2019), and *Trees and Thorns: Studies in the First Chapters of Genesis* (West Monroe, LA: Athansius Press, 2020), etc.

[2] The word "שבכ" (subdue) is only used fifteen times in the Old Testament (Gen. 1:28; Num. 32:22, 29; Josh. 18:1; 2 Sam. 8:11; Jer. 34:11, 16; Mic. 7:19; Zech. 9:15; Esth. 7:8; Neh. 5:5; 1 Chr. 22:18; 2 Chr. 28:10). The use in Genesis 1:28 is obviously unique, given the context.

is no implication in the creation narrative that man and the creation are at war or that man subdues the world by violence, for the world is in complete harmony and all is very good before the fall (Gen. 1:31).

The eschatological picture suggested here is that of a world filled with God's image benevolently ruling the creation and leading all creatures into a fullness of fruit-bearing and blessing. The fall of man introduced complications to this, but the rest of the Bible details how this original commission finds its ultimate fulfillment. Thus, we must note that the fall did not nullify the blessing given to Adam and his wife, for the same commission—with significant additions—is given to Noah and his sons, again as a covenant "blessing" (Gen. 9:1-7). God's original plan moves forward, in spite of sin and Satan.

The rebellion in Eden brought death into the world, leading to the proliferation of sin. The rebellion at the tower of Babel brought deep division into the families of mankind—another form of death. When Yahweh called Abram, He promised that through Abram all the families of the earth would be blessed, implying that both the fall and Babel would be overcome through God's covenant grace. Abram had to become Abraham (Gen. 17:5), receive the covenant sign of circumcision (Gen. 17:9-14) and, in his dead state (Heb. 11:11-12), be given his covenant son, Isaac (Gen. 21:1-7), before he could even see the beginning of the fulfillment of the promises. But he did see the beginning, and his descendant Joseph ruled the world and brought blessing to the seed of Abraham and the nations. The book of Genesis ends with a typological fulfillment of the promises that points forward to the end, when Abraham's greater Son sits on a greater throne to bring eternal blessing—but that is getting ahead of the story.

Yahweh's covenant promise to Abraham—renewed and expanded repeatedly throughout the Old Testament, especially in the covenant with David— showed that the Adamic mandate had never been abrogated. Even more, Jesus' Great Commission to the church showed how it would be fulfilled. Jesus brought in a New Covenant to fulfill all that the old covenant promised and foreshadowed, including filling the world with God's image and subduing all things to bring glory to God.

In the Great Commission (Matt. 28:18-10), Jesus commanded His disciples to "disciple"—a verb in Greek—"all the nations" (the direct object of the verb "disciple."[3] In other words, Jesus' disciples are command-

---

[3] I cannot resist making reference here to Hal Lindsey's "exegesis" of Jesus' command, not just because it is an example of gross distortion of the text of Scripture by a man who majored in Greek at a well-known seminary, but more because it illustrates the way almost all modern evangelicals actually read the text. Lindsey wrote: "Go therefore and make disciples of [Greek = *out of*] all the nations. . . . We are told to make disciples from out of all the Gentiles. You don't disciple nations, you disciple individuals, so the Greek word translated *nations* should be understood in its most frequently used sense—*Gentiles*." The irony here is deep. Jesus actually commanded us to do what Lindsey said cannot be done: "disciple all the nations." If we would translate the word as "Gentiles," as Lindsey suggests, it really doesn't change anything, for the command would then be, "disciple all Gentiles." What Lindsey needs for his approach, and what most evangelicals assume, is the missing Greek word "out of" [Greek = *out of*]. The tragedy/irony for Lindsey's exegesis is that the

ed to "subdue" all the nations of the world—"subdue" to Christ through the Gospel. The Great Commission is a command to world conquest: not merely political—though that as well—but first of all spiritual and covenantal, a conquest of the heart and soul of individuals, families, and nations. Thus, Jesus' ambition is far greater than that of Alexander the Great, Genghis Kahn, or Caesar! Of course, His method of world conquest is totally different from theirs.

> But Jesus called them to Himself and said to them, "You know that those who are considered rulers over the Gentiles lord it over them, and their great ones exercise authority over them. Yet it shall not be so among you; but whoever desires to become great among you shall be your servant. And whoever of you desires to be first shall be slave of all. For even the Son of Man did not come to be served, but to serve, and to give His life a ransom for many." (Mark 10:42-45)

He called His disciples to take up the cross and follow Him, to lose their lives to bear fruit for life eternal (Mark 8:34; John 12:24-26).

Greek simply does not say "make disciples of." There is no "Greek = out of!" To repeat, "disciple" in the Greek is a verb with a direct object, "all the nations." Hal Lindsey, *The Road to Holocaust* (New York: Bantam Books, 1989), 49. See also my, *The Baptism of Jesus the Christ* (Eugene, Oregon: Wipf & Stock, 2010), 197-98.

The subjugation of the world is to be accomplished as the Great Commission commands: First, by baptism into the Name of the Father and the Son and the Holy Spirit. Why baptism? Because baptism is a covenant-oath ceremony, bringing the baptized individuals and nations into submission to the Lordship of the Messiah Jesus, carrying with it abundant promises and assurance of God's love and grace.[4] Second, by teaching the nations to obey "all things" that Jesus commanded. Baptism introduces the nations into the New Covenant, teaching nations, families, and individuals to obey, showing them how to live the life of the New Covenant, thereby enabling them to exercise righteous dominion over whatever stewardship God has granted to them.

The Great Commission, therefore, presupposes and completes the vision of the original covenant command given to Adam in the Garden and repeated to Noah after the flood. It aims at the fulfillment of the eschatology implied in creation. But there is an aspect of the Great Commission that neither Abraham or anyone else in the

---

[4] The command to disciple the nations is defined in the most basic terms in the Great Commission. First, people must be baptized *into* the name (singular) of the Father and the Son and the Holy Spirit. The importance of the word "into" is often missed because of being translated as "in." Carson explains it well: "Matthew, unlike some NT writers, apparently avoids the confusion of *eis* (strictly "into") and *en* (strictly "in"; cf. Zerwick, *Biblical Greek*, para. 106) common in Hellenistic Greek; if so, the preposition "into" strongly suggests a coming-into-relationship-with or a coming-under-the-lordship-of . . . . It is a sign both of entrance into Messiah's covenant community and of pledged submission to his lordship." Carson, *Matthew* (The Expositor's Bible Commentary).

old covenant era would have anticipated and that Jesus' own disciples never imagined in the years before His resurrection: the eschatology of the creation implied the incarnation of the Son of God.

There are difficulties in articulating this matter which are related to debates in Reformed theology. I am referring to arguments about "infralapsarianism" and "supralapsarianism," or debates about the order of God's decrees.[5] As Bavinck expounds at length, all orthodox Christians from Augustine, through Aquinas, to Luther and Calvin onward, have always believed that God ordains all things that come to pass. The Bible is too clear on the subject to escape the basic truth of God's sovereignty: "In Him also we have obtained an inheritance, being predestined according to the purpose of Him who works all things according to the counsel of His will" (Eph. 1:11).

Also, no one imagines that God's plan was put together piecemeal, as if there could be an "order" of decrees that exhibited God's thinking process, a temporal order of decision making. Rather the debate is about the *logical* order of the decrees. Bavinck sums it up: "The key issue here is whether to consider the decree to elect and to reprobate logically before (supra-) or after (infra-) the decree to create and to permit the fall."[6] Bavnck's conclusion is that there is truth in both positions, but that "neither the supralapsarian nor the infralapsarian view

---

[5] See especially, Herman Bavinck, *Reformed Dogmatics: Volume 2: God and Creation* (Grand Rapids: Baker Academic, 2004), 361-66 and 388-92.

[6] Ibid.

of predestination is capable of incorporating within its perspective the fullness and riches of the truth of Scripture and of satisfying our theological thinking."[7] Though we can only consider things one at a time, God "surveys the whole world-historical scene. All things are eternally present to his consciousness. His counsel is one single conception, one in which all the particular decrees are arranged in the same interconnected pattern in which, a posteriori, the facts of history in part appear to us to be arranged now and will one day appear to be fully arranged."[8] He continues:

> This interconnected pattern is so enormously rich and complex that it cannot be reproduced in a single word such as "infralapsarian" or "supralapsarian." It is both causally and teleologically connected. Preceding components impact subsequent components, but even future events already condition the past and the present. The whole picture is marked by immensely varied omnilateral interaction. Accordingly, predestination in the ordinary sense of the word as the foreordination of the eternal state of rational creatures and of the steps leading to that state, is not the one all-encompassing decree of God. While it is an utterly significant part of the counsel of God, it does not coincide with it. The counsel of God is the master concept

---

[7] Ibid.

[8] Ibid.

because it is comprehensive. It covers all things without exception: heaven and earth, spirit and matter, things visible and invisible, creatures animate and inanimate. It is the one will of God governing the whole cosmos, past, present, and future.[9]

It is appropriate to keep in mind Bavinck's perspective on the infra-supra debate when we ask a related question: Would the Son of God have become incarnate even without the fall? Even if Adam had not sinned, is it possible that the Son would have become a man? If we answer, "Yes," to this question, we are suggesting that there was a deeper and prior purpose to the incarnation: the union of God and man. Surely the Son became man to save His people from their sins, but was that the ultimate purpose in the plan of God?

Since the Bible does indicate that the Son had to take on flesh and blood in order to save us from sin (Heb. 2:14-18), some Christians will regard the question as overly speculative at best. The explicit declaration of Scripture is clear, why speculate? James Jordan, on the other hand, believes the question is important, even essential. He puts it directly: "Would Christ have come into the world if Adam had not sinned?" His response is equally unequivocal: "The answer is clearly 'yes.'"

How can he make such a positive assertion on a matter that is by no means settled in the history of theological discourse? He explains:

---

[9] Ibid.

It is often thought that the only reason the Son of God became incarnate was to deal with Adam's sin. Most people do not think this through. If they did, they would realize that it is a problematic idea, for it means that the only reason humanity becomes the Bride of Christ is because of the fall of Adam. And this means that the fall was a good thing. The notion that the fall was a good thing is called the doctrine or heresy of the felicitous fall.[10]

Further:

But there is a conflict of categories when we say that God absolutely predestinated the fall of man in order to bring about the "morally" good result of the incarnation. If God "wanted," in the moral sense, for His Son to come into the world and be the Husband of humanity, and the only way this could happen was for man to rebel, then God "wanted," in the moral sense, for man to fall. To put it another way, this position says that the *only* way God could bring about the wonderful Divine-Human marriage of His only-begotten Son and His created daughter was by means of predestinating the rebellion of that daughter.

---

[10] *Federal Vision*, Kindle Version.

This, I submit, is intolerable.[11]

Let's take just a moment to think about this. What Jordan regards as "intolerable" has not always been, or rather, not usually been regarded so. For example, in *Paradise Lost*, Milton has Adam reflect upon the blessings of salvation that have come from his sin.

> That all this good of evil shall produce,
> And evil turn to good—more wonderful
> Than that which by creation first—brought
>   forth
> Light out of darkness! full of doubt I stand,
> Whether I should repent me now of sin
> By me done or occasioned, or rejoice
> Much more that much more good thereof shall
>   spring
> To God more glory, more good will to men
> From God-and over wrath grace shall abound[12]

Poor Adam cannot decide whether to repent or not! If his sin was the necessary condition for the incarnation, the dilemma is real. Without Adam's sin, the Son would not become a man and there would never be a new race of man in Christ to be united with God. To sin or not

---

[11] Ibid.

[12] John Milton, *Paradise Lost,* Book 12, Line 470-479. The quotation above follows the updated spelling in Arthur Lovejoy, "Milton and the Paradox of the Fortunate Fall" in *A Journal of English Literary History,* vol. 4, no. 3, September 1937, 161-62.

to sin! Who could answer the question? Or, rather, given the wonderful outcome of the matter, who would not, in the end, come down on the side of rejoicing in the result rather than repenting of the sin?

The "paradox" expressed in Milton was not at all new, for it was found in theological exposition at least from the time of Ambrose. In fact, the "felicitous fall" was not only expressed in theological treatises and sermons. The "*felix culpa*" appeared in a *devotional hymn* in the Roman Liturgy, perhaps from as early as the fourth century, in the *Exsultet*.

> O certe necessarium Adae peccatum,
> quod Christi morte deletum est!
> O felix culpa,
> quae talem ac tantum meruit habere redemptorem!

> O truly necessary sin of Adam,
> destroyed completely by the Death of Christ!
> O happy fault
> that earned for us so great, so glorious a Redeemer![13]

One of the most extreme statements of the "felicitous fall" comes in the "most famous and widely read" Roman Catholic devotional by St. Francis de Sales, *Traite de l'amour de Dieu.*

---

[13] Wikipedia gives both the Latin and the English translation. https://en.wikipedia.org/wiki/Exsultet. The article by Lovejoy cited above gives the same original and translation, as well as a thorough summary of the history of the idea.

Therefore the Church, in a holy excess of admiration, exclaims on the Eve of Easter: "O sin of Adam, truly necessary" etc. [quotes the two sentences from the *Exultet*]. Of a truth, we can say with that man of ancient times: "We should be lost (*perdus*) if we had not been lost;" that is to say, our loss has been our gain, since human nature has received more gifts of grace (*plus de graces*) from its redemption by its Savior than it would ever have received from the innocence of Adam, if he had persevered in it. . . . The Angels, the Savior tells us, "have more joy over one sinner that repenteth than over ninety and-nine just persons that need no repentance;" and in the same way, the state of redemption is one hundred times greater in value than the state of innocence.[14]

What de Sales explicitly pronounces is implicit in any other version of the "felicitous fall:" that for the sake of the human race it was better for Adam to have sinned—far better, infinitely better—than for him to have obeyed God and remained innocent!

Jordan is correct. This view—though common in church history—is intolerable. But what other view is there? The alternative view—that the incarnation was not logically dependent upon the fall—has been called

---

[14] Quotation from Lovejoy, "Milton and the Paradox of the Fortunate Fall," 178.

"Supralapsarian Christology."[15] As we saw above, Jordan explains that even apart from the fall, the Son would have become man because God's ultimate purpose for the creation of man was not dependent on the fall. The fall was truly a fall, not a benefit in disguise. Contrary to de Sales and an ancient tradition, the biblical account unequivocally assumes that Adam would have been better off—not to mention his posterity—if he had remained in the state of innocence.

What might the world have been then? Van Driel offers help with his Christology. He suggests that there are three lines of argument for supralapsarian Christology: ". . . each of the three ways in which God is taken to relate to what is not God—in creation, in redemption, and in eschatological consummation—can function as the basis for a supralapsarian argument."[16] To slightly modify his three ways, I suggest: 1) narrative of creation; 2) the history of redemption; 3) the eschatological consummation. I begin with consummation and work my way back to creation, for we have to assume that God planned things with an end in view and since He has revealed that end to us, we have to reflect on the whole history of the world in the light of that end.

---

[15] "We can call such an understanding of the incarnation supralapsarian: the divine will to become incarnate logically precedes (supra, before) the divine will to allow sin." Edwin Chr. Van Driel, *Incarnation Anyway: Arguments for Supralapsarian Christology* (Oxford: Oxford University Press, 2008), 40-41.

[16] Edwin Chr. Van Driel, *Incarnation Anyway: Arguments for Supralapsarian Christology* (Oxford: Oxford University Press, 2008), 42-43.

In his *The Biblical Philosophy of History*, R. J. Rushdoony stated a basic principle that indicates the importance of considering the eschatological dimension first.

> Biblical philosophy of history means that time does not come out of a primeval past, but from eternity. The origin of time is not in chaos but in eternity. Evolutionary time emerges out of the past, gropes its way blindly into the present, and moves sightlessly into an unknown future. The movement of time is thus from the past to the present into the future. The movement of time, according to the Bible, is from eternity, since it is created by God and moves out of and in terms of His eternal decree. Because time moves in terms of the eternal decree, when its function is finished there shall be time no more (Rev. 10:6). Because time is predestined, and because its beginning and end are already established, time does not develop in evolutionary fashion from past to present to future. Instead, it unfolds from future to present to past. In Wood's words, "The future is the source, it is the reservoir of time which some day will be present, and then past." Better stated, eternity is the source; time is predestined, and therefore it moves from the future to the present to the past. "The future is logically first, but not chronologically."[17]

---

[17] Rousas John Rushdoony, *The Biblical Philosophy of History* (Val-

The future source of the movement of history, the goal which pulls history in its direction, is seen throughout the New Testament Gospels and epistles because the Bible is an emphatically eschatological book. We can only consider two passages, and them only superficially. First, Jesus' prayer in John 17 reveals in relatively straightforward language what the book of Revelation depicts in vision—a climax of history in which God and man, as well as man and man, have all become one in God's covenantal grace. In His high priestly prayer, Jesus prayed that the new race of mankind in Him—the people that He describes as those that the Father has given Him—should be perfectly united, even as He and the Father are one. Jesus is obviously not praying for ontological oneness among humans, for He predicates human oneness on the indwelling of the Father and Son: "I in them, and You in Me; that they may be made perfect in one" (17:23, cf. vs. 21, 26). Since all of those whom the Father has given to Jesus will be indwelt by both Father and Son, they will be covenantally one with the Triune God and therefore with one another.[18]

In the Triune God, mutual indwelling is the definition of ontological oneness and *also* the meaning of covenantal oneness. Ontology and covenant are one in God because the covenantal relations of the Three Persons define who God Himself is. He cannot be other than Father, Son, and Spirit in an eternal fellowship of love.

---

lecito, CA: Ross House Books, 1969), 9.

[18] Note: This is both individual and collective eschatology since Jesus is praying for each one and all.

But in God's relationship with creation, covenant and ontology are *not* one—just as the deity and humanity of Christ are fundamentally distinguished, not ontologically one because Creator and creature are ontologically and absolutely distinct.

God and creation cannot be ontologically one. However, God can be covenantally united with man, His created image. What does that mean? God's image as a race of mankind cannot be ontologically one like God because of the absolute separation between Creator and creature, but we can share in the covenantal oneness that comes from being indwelt by Father, Son, and Spirit. Indeed, that oneness with God and sharing in the fellowship of the Trinity is the ultimate purpose of God's creating mankind and leading history to its climax in the descent of the New Jerusalem to earth.

In the book of Revelation, John sees heaven and earth united as the Bride of Christ comes down to earth as God's tabernacle, His eternal dwelling place with man (21:2-3). The New Covenant finds its realization in a new tabernacle, as God and man are united in bliss—no more death, no more sorrow, no more pain and crying (21:4). The glory of God and the Lamb of God illumine the city with everlasting light that drives away night forever. The glorious picture of history's eschatological climax is grounded in the incarnation; it is the fulfillment of the Son's incarnation. It cannot be anything other than the very purpose of the Son's incarnation, a purpose that cannot be dependent upon Adam rebelling against God, for that would subordinate the vision of the New Jerusalem to the "*felix culpa*" (happy fall). If God's ultimate purpose were logically subordinated to the fall, then Adam's part in our salvation is hardly less important than Christ's!

The history of redemption points also to the priority of the incarnation, for if Adam's sin is the prerequisite for final glory, the history of redemption would be seen in the same light—Adam's imitators from Cain, to Nimrod, to Ahab and a thousand others all sinned against God in order that He might bring blessing out of the mess they created. Without their corruption, the blessings of grace could not come.

But if the incarnation is the beginning and end of God's leading the world to a climax of love and unity, then the repeated falls in history are not repetitions of an Adamic "*felix culpa,*" but part of the story of God building His kingdom *in spite of sin and rebellion* because from the beginning He was aiming at incarnation and ultimate oneness between God and man in the New Jerusalem. The whole history of redemption points forward to the climax.

So also does the creation of the world. Though God did indeed plan for Adam to fall, the plan for the incarnation was not *logically* conditioned upon the decree of the fall. I cannot begin to summarize the book *Trees and Thorns,* except to say that Jordan's exposition of the first four chapters of Genesis presents a narrative introduction to the Bible in which every aspect of the story points forward to the incarnation of the Son as the ultimate purpose and meaning of man being created as God's image. The eschatological climax that was typologically manifested throughout covenant history, that Jesus prayed for and John prophesied in Revelation was present in seed form before the fall.

In conclusion, considering the relationship of the fall to biblical eschatology brings us back to Jordan's definition of "covenant:" "*The Covenant is a personal-structural bond which joins the three Persons of God in a community of life, and in which man was created to participate.*"[19] Jordan's definition of the covenant presupposes the eschatological end Jesus prayed for: God and man, and man and man, being united in covenantal oneness. God's creation plan and purpose was this ultimate covenantal unity of life and love: Father, Son, and Spirit indwelling Christ's church and the church as a truly unified body revealing the glory of her Head!

---

[19] James B. Jordan, *The Law of the Covenant: An Exposition of Exodus 21-23* (Tyler, Tex.: Institute for Christian Economics, 1984), 5. Italics in original. Hoeksema's definition is similar: "The idea of the covenant is certainly not that of a pact or an agreement, whether you conceive of such an agreement in the unilateral or bilateral sense. *The covenant is the relation of the most intimate communion of friendship, in which God reflects his own covenant life in his relation to the creature, gives to that creature life, and causes him to taste and acknowledge the highest good and the overflowing fountain of all good.*" Op. cit. Italics in original.

CHAPTER 8

CONCLUSION

Eric Auerbach's monumental study of the representation of reality in Western literature, *Mimesis*, begins with
a chapter titled "Odysseus' Scar," which contrasts book
nineteen of Homer's Odyssey to the biblical story of the
sacrifice of Isaac in Genesis 22. Auerbach wrote:

> It would be difficult, then, to imagine styles
> more contrasted than those of these two equal-
> ly ancient and equally epic texts. On the one
> hand, externalized, uniformly illuminated phe-
> nomena, at a definite time and in a definite
> place, connected together without lacunae in
> a perpetual foreground; thoughts and feeling
> completely expressed; events taking place in lei-
> surely fashion and with very little of suspense.
> On the other hand, the externalization of only

so much of the phenomena as is necessary for the purpose of the narrative, all else left in obscurity; the decisive points of the narrative alone are emphasized, what lies between is non-existent; time and place are undefined and call for interpretation; thoughts and feeling remain unexpressed, are only suggested by the silence and the fragmentary speeches; the whole, permeated with the most unrelieved suspense and directed toward a single goal (and to that extent far more of a unity), remains mysterious and "fraught with background."[1]

Auerbach, a secular German Jew, writing in Istanbul, while in exile from Nazi Germany, had no glimpse of the background which haunts the biblical narrative, the unexpressed mystery that permeates and unifies what may seem like fragmentary stories. Peter Leithart, expounding the story of creation in Genesis 1, enables us to hear the partially hidden Trinitarian dimensions of the story.[2] Long before the truth of the Trinity was revealed in the events of incarnation of the Son and the gift of the Spirit, the Father, Son, and Spirit built the world in covenantal love and harmony.

---

[1] Erich Auerbach, *Mimesis: The Representation of Reality in Western Literature* (Princeton, NJ: Princeton University Press, Fiftieth-Anniversary Edition, 2003), 11-12.

[2] Peter Leithart, "Triune Creator," Theopolis Institute, https://theopolisinstitute.com/conversations/triune-creator/.

In this book, by putting together themes and ideas from writings by Kuyper, Van Til, Jordan, Leithart and others, I have argued that the truth of the Triune God's eternal covenant relationship is the archetypical background for the biblical idea of the covenant and the outworking of God's covenantal relationship with mankind from Genesis to Revelation. Quotations and footnotes include many theologians and writers who would not necessarily agree with my project or who might even be appalled by it, but in various expressions I find in them an affinity they might not perceive. The mystery of the Triune God Himself draws all Christians to meditate on His Person, and we often express our partial insights in similar language.

Jordan's near starting point seems to have been Cornelius Van Til, who himself realized his debts to others, writing, "Standing on the shoulders of Warfield and Kuyper we honor them best if we build on the main thrust of their thought rather than if we insist on carrying on what is inconsistent with their basic position. Then are we most faithful to Calvin and to St. Paul."[3] As a faithful

---

[3] Cornelius Van Til, *The Defense of the Faith* (Logos Library System), 252. Van Til's entire book is devoted, among other things, to defend his faithfulness to the Reformed tradition, especially to Abraham Kuyper, but Warfield and others as well. In *A Christian Theory of Knowledge*, Van Til wrote: "The writer is therefore greatly indebted to the great Reformed exegetes of Scripture. In modern times many excellent commentaries written by Reformed scholars have appeared. He is also greatly indebted to the great Reformed dogmaticians of modern times, such as Charles Hodge, Thornwell, Dabney, Shedd, Kuyper and especially Herman Bavinck. Back of all of them stands that master theologian and exegete of Scripture, John Calvin, whose

heir to a great tradition, Van Til sought to build upon it, adding to the edifice that had already been set up over the centuries.

Van Til himself was blessed with many faithful heirs. John Frame and Vern Poythress stand out among them because they lock arms as brothers in expounding the Trinitarian dimensions of Van Til's thought, explicating perspectives on the Trinitarian nature of all reality.[4] James Jordan is unique, I think, among Van Til's heirs in seeking to expound the biblical worldview in the unfamiliar—to modern men—categories of the Bible.

The Biblical worldview is not given to us in the discursive and analytical language of philosophy and science, but in the rich and compact language of symbolism and art. It is pictured in ritual and architecture, in numerical structures and geographical directions, in symbols and types, in trees and stars. In short, it is given to

---

writings have been constantly consulted." (Logos Library System), 2. John Frame outlines more fully the influences on Van Til's thought in Cornelius *Van Til: An Analysis of His Thought* (Phillipsburg, NJ: Presbyterian and Reformed Publishing, 1995), especially in Chapter Two, 24-26.

[4] See: https://frame-poythress.org/ The website, which includes free books and essays in abundance, is titled: "Tri-perspectival Theology for the Church." See also Timothy E. Miller, *The Triune God of Unity in Diversity: An Analysis of Perspectivalism, the Trinitarian Theological Method of John Frame and Vern Poythress* (Phillipsburg, NJ: P&R Publishing, 2017).

us in a premodern package that seems at places very strange.[5]

Similar to the brotherly labor of Frame and Poythress, James Jordan and Peter Leithart strive together to build on the foundations provided by the Christian tradition they have inherited, including but not limited to the broad tradition of Reformed theology. Readers of this book—if there are any!—will not find in Jordan and Leithart tedious repetition and reference to Trinity and covenant, which someone might fear or expect from reading this book. On the contrary, their exposition of who the Triune God is and how He works in creation, history, and redemption finds copious expression in books and essays that cover a wide range of topics—none of it tedious, much of it almost breathtaking. Among their commentaries, Jordan's work on Daniel[6] and Leithart's work on Revelation[7] deserve special mention as works of superb scholarship based on humble and zealous faith in the Triune God.

This book has attempted to elucidate what might be called a sometimes explicit, but always reverberating "background" to what Jordan and Leithart—and many others influenced by them—have written and taught. It

---

[5] *Through New Eyes* (Brentwood, TN: Wolgemuth & Hyatt, 1989), 1.

[6] *The Handwriting on the Wall: A Commentary on the Book of Daniel* (Powder Springs, GA: American Vision, 2007).

[7] Peter J. Leithart, *Revelation 1-11* (London: Bloomsbury T & T Clark, 2018) and *Revelation 12-22* (London: Bloomsbury T & T Clark, 2018).

will be a success as a book if it encourages readers to follow their exhortations to reform Christian worship of the Triune covenantal God, to practice weekly communion that includes covenant children and to sing the Psalms with vigor.

THE FOUNDATION OF THE TRINITARIAN COVENANT

This appendix is a more detailed argument for the foundation of the covenant presented in chapter one.

To consider the covenantal relationships among the Persons of the Trinity, we need to ask the basic question: What does that expression mean? What do we mean by saying "covenantal relationships among the Persons of the Trinity"? I mean that Father, Son, and Spirit share an eternal covenantal bond of love, a covenantal bond essential to Trinitarian existence. To repeat for emphasis, contrary to the common reformed definition of covenant, the covenant I am speaking of is not a "contract" or "agreement" into which the Persons of the Trinity entered.[1] As I pointed out in the introduction, the covenantal bond I am speaking of is an aspect of who the Triune God is— *covenant as Trinitarian ontology.*

The idea that the Persons of the Trinity relate in covenant is not widely acknowledged, even among those who believe in what is called "covenant theology" and place great emphasis on the importance of Biblical covenants.[2]

---

[1] Note also, the Torah of Moses cannot be rightly understood as a "contract," "agreement," or "treaty," though it is certainly a covenant. The Torah as a written document expresses the instruction of Israel's loving Father, Yahweh, for His son. It certainly includes "statutes, ordinances, and commandments," but it cannot be reduced to a set of rules followed by curses for disobedience and blessings for obedience. The statutes, ordinances, and commandments include paradoxically expressed instruction similar to Wisdom literature. They are full of ceremonial instruction and symbolism. They express Yahweh's love and set out Yahweh's way of love, calling Israel to imitate Him. The covenant that Yahweh gave to Israel was His way to draw near to her and allow her to draw near to Him. In other words, the Mosaic covenant is one in a series of graciously-given covenants that express Yahweh's love for His people. See my, *Hear, My Son: An Examination of the Fatherhood of Yahweh in Deuteronomy* (Monroe, LA: Athanasius Press, 2011).

[2] Jeffrey J. Niehaus outlines various views of covenants in the Bible in his, "An Argument Against Theologically Constructed Covenants" in *The Journal of the Evangelical Theological Society*, no. 50/2, June 2007. It is telling that in the same article Niehaus critiques William Dumbrell's view that biblical covenants are the expression of one covenant in these words: "It should be clear by now that Dumbrell has blurred the categories of covenant and covenant renewal. He does so because he has not developed an understanding of these categories from a study of ancient Near Eastern sources." Ignoring for the moment that Dumbrell's various works show sufficient knowledge of the ancient Near East, consider what Niehaus implies: if we do

Perhaps the main reason an intra-trinitarian covenant is not usually recognized is that, like the doctrine of the Trinity itself, it does not come to direct expression or exposition in the Bible. An intra-trinitarian covenant is an inference from what the Bible teaches us about God and what the Bible shows us about His relationships with the world He has created. This is most natural. Note: in the same way that a fully stated trinitarian doctrine cannot be found in any specific place in the Bible, the doctrine of an intra-trinitarian covenant is not based on a single prooftext or collection of prooftexts.[3]

---

not study ancient Near Eastern sources, we cannot adequately understand the Bible and its teaching about covenants. Bad news for the first nineteen-hundred years of church history! I believe, on the contrary, that unless we know the history revealed in Genesis 1-11, we cannot have a properly developed understanding of the ancient Near East. With a perspective similar to Niehaus, Jonathan S. Greer, John W. Hilber, and John H. Walton edited a book titled *Behind the Scenes of the Old Testament: Cultural, Social, and Historical Contexts* (Grand Rapids, Baker Academic, 2018). This reveals a fundamentally wrong approach. As I also point out in the appendix, it is actually Genesis 1-11 that takes us behind the scenes of all human history and shows us the sources and context for ancient Near Eastern culture and society.

[3] Benjamin Warfield wrote: "The doctrine of the Trinity lies in Scripture in solution; when it is crystallized from its solvent it does not cease to be Scriptural, but only comes into clearer view. Or, to speak without figure, the doctrine of the Trinity is given to us in Scripture, not in formulated definition, but in fragmentary allusions; when we assemble the *disjecta membra* into their organic unity, we are not passing from Scripture, but entering more thoroughly into the meaning of Scripture. We may state the doctrine in technical terms, supplied by philosophical reflection; but the doctrine stated is a genuinely Scriptural doctrine." Benjamin B. Warfield, "Trinity"

What then is the foundation of the idea of a Trinitarian covenant? Its foundation is, in fact, the same as one of the most important aspects of trinitarian theology. Herman Bavinck expressed it well: "The ontological Trinity is reflected in the economical Trinity."[4] What Bavinck here calls the "economical Trinity" refers to God as He reveals Himself in the works of creation and redemption. What he calls the "ontological Trinity" refers to God as He is in Himself from eternity, apart from His relationships to all that is not God.

A full statement of the doctrine of the Trinity requires us to reason from the economy to the ontology. We can only know who God is in Himself by considering His self-revelation in His words and works from creation to new creation. In fact, as Benjamin Warfield pointed out: "We cannot speak of the doctrine of the Trinity, therefore, if we study exactness of speech, as revealed in the New Testament, any more than we can speak of it as revealed in the Old Testament. The Old Testament was written before its revelation; the New Testament after it. The revelation itself was made not in word but in deed. It was made in the incarnation of God the Son, and the outpouring

---

in *The International Standard Bible Encyclopedia,* vol. 5, ed. James Or (Grand Rapids: Eerdmans, 1939), 435.

[4] Herman Bavinck, *The Doctrine of God* (Edinburgh: Banner of Truth Trust, 1977), 317. Bavinck's statement of the relationship between the economic Trinity and the ontological Trinity is far superior to Karl Rahner's. See Ralph Allan Smith, "Against Karl Rahner's Rule." https://www.berith.org/pdf/against-karl-rahner-s-rule.pdf

of God the Holy Spirit."[5] Thus, "Our New Testament is not a record of the development of the doctrine or of its assimilation. It everywhere presupposes the doctrine as the fixed possession of the Christian community; and the process by which it became the possession of the Christian community lies behind the New Testament."[6]

Similarly, though not with the same clarity or emphasis, the doctrine of an intra-trinitarian covenant was not revealed in the Old Testament, though it was prepared for in the way God created the world and led history. Nor is the idea of an intra-trinitarian covenant expressly revealed in the New Testament. However, the doctrine is clearly hinted at in a number of passages and may be said to be universally presupposed. Unless we infer Trinitarian truth on every page of Scripture—which is from beginning to the end a covenantal Word—we cannot comprehend New Testament language about God or think correctly about His covenants with mankind.

Though Thomas Torrance does not here speak of the gift of a covenant relationship, his comments about God's work in history are relevant:

> It is certainly true that our theological conceptions of God as Father, Son and Holy Spirit derive from and are essentially coordinated with what God has manifested of himself in the historical events of which we read in the New Testament. Those evangelical events are empty

---

[5] Warfield, op. cit., 444.

[6] Ibid.

if they are sundered from their roots in history. They have saving import for us only if the historical presentations of God as Father, Son and Holy Spirit flow from and direct us back to personal realities inside the divine Life. *That is to say, the historical manifestations of God as Father, Son and Holy Spirit have evangelical and theological significance only as they have a transhistorical and transfinite reference beyond to an ultimate ground in God himself.* They cannot be Gospel if their reference breaks off at the finite boundaries of this world of space and time, for as such they would be empty of divine validity and saving significance—that would be to leave us trapped in some kind of historical positivism. The historical manifestations of the Trinity are Gospel, however, if they are grounded beyond history in the eternal personal distinctions between the Father, the Son and the Holy Spirit inherent in the Godhead, that is, if the Fatherhood of the Father, the Sonship of the Son, and the Communion of the Spirit belong to the inner Life of God and constitute his very Being.[7]

If we can only know God as He has revealed Himself in history—which includes verbal revelation, of course—then consider God's work in history. What do we see? It is undeniably patent that one of God's most characteristic

---

[7] Thomas F. Torrance, *The Christian Doctrine of God, One Being Three Persons* (London: Bloomsbury T&T Clark, 2016), 6. Italics added.

acts is to enter into a covenant relationship with men, or, rather, to graciously bestow His covenant to men. The pressing question is, why? Why should God always and everywhere relate to man in and by covenants? What is it about a "covenant" that makes it so special in God's relationships with mankind—His image and likeness?

In fact, we must say that even before man was created, God "covenanted" with the whole world since He created the world in a covenantal fashion.[8] What does "covenantal fashion" mean? The remarkably strange—"unscientific"?—process described in Genesis—creating the world through commandments, evaluating what came into being, and blessing the creation—is a *covenantal* process. Obviously, it is not the only way that God could have created the world and it is such an extraordinary way of creating that we have to ask what is going on. When we consider the process described in Genesis in the light of the rest of biblical revelation, it is clear that we see the very first gift of a covenant—even a Trinitarian

---

[8] See: James B. Jordan, *Creation in Six Days: A Defense of the Traditional Reading of Genesis One* (Moscow, ID: Canon Press, 1999), 173, "The creation narrative describes God's making the world over the course of a week. God's work is cosmic and covenantal. The language in Genesis 1 is used in covenant-making events later on in the Bible . . ." In renewing the covenant relationship with Noah, God specifically includes animals: "And as for Me, behold, I establish My covenant with you and with your descendants after you, and with every living creature that *is* with you: the birds, the cattle, and every beast of the earth with you, of all that go out of the ark, every beast of the earth" (Gen. 9:9-10), implying that God's relationship with all creation was covenantal from the beginning—and also certainly not an "agreement"!

covenant.[9] The absolute authority of the Lord comes to expression in His command. Obedience by the creature and blessing by God show the whole creation narrative to be a covenant-making story. The question is, to reiterate, why should God create the world in this manner?

Add to that, as we pointed out briefly above: why should God establish covenants with Adam, Noah, Abraham, Israel, David, and post-exilic Judah? Why did Jesus make a "new covenant" for the salvation of His people? Consider: the word "covenant" appears over three hundred times in the English Bible! But more than that, the centrality of the covenant for God's relationship with mankind is most clearly seen in that all humans are either "in Adam" or "in Christ"—obviously not a statement about "physical relationships!" Adam and Christ are two covenant heads who lead in very different directions (Rom. 5:12 ff.; 1 Cor. 15:22).

With all this and more in mind, many Reformed theologians, though not all, have posited an eternal covenant between the Father and the Son[10] for the salvation of the elect, called "the covenant of redemption," "the *pactum salutis*,"[11] or "the counsel of peace."[12]

---

[9] Peter J. Leithart, "Triune Creator," Theopolis Institute, https://theopolisinstitute.com/conversations/triune-creator/.

[10] The Spirit is sometimes left out of the formula as explicitly stated.

[11] Kostenberger and Swain discuss the *pactum salutis* in explaining Jesus' prayer in John 17. Andreas J. Kostenberger and Scott R. Swain, *Father, Son and Spirit: The Trinity and John's Gospel* (Downers Grove, IL: InterVarsity Press, 2008), 169ff.

[12] The history of this is complicated, as Bavinck shows. "In the Re-

On the one hand, the inference that salvation is grounded in an eternal agreement among the Persons of the Trinity provides what Bavinck called practical encouragement for Christian living. Also, the fact that we read of Father, Son, and Spirit "consulting" to make man—"Let us make man in our image"—implies that the Persons of the Trinity "converse" in eternity as well. In fact, Geerhardus Vos[13] and Herman Bavinck have a profoundly high view of the *pactum salutis*: "In the decrees, also in those of predestination, the one will of God occupied the foreground, and their trinitarian character was still blurred. But here, in the pact of salvation, the work of redemption

---

formed church and theology, covenant became a very important practical encouragement for Christian living. Here the basis of all covenants was found in the eternal counsel of God, in a covenant between the very persons of the Trinity, the *pactum salutis* (counsel of peace). The work of salvation is an undertaking of the one God in three persons in which all cooperate and each one performs a special task." Also, "As a result of all this, Scripture offers us a multifaceted and glorious picture of the work of redemption. The pact of salvation makes known to us the relationships and life of the three persons in the Divine Being as a covenantal life, a life of consummate self-consciousness and freedom. Here, within the Divine Being, the covenant flourishes to the full." Excerpts from: Herman Bavinck. "Reformed Dogmatics Volume 3: Sin & Salvation in Christ." Apple Books.

[13] Geerhardus Vos, *Redemptive History and Biblical Interpretation: The Shorter Writings of Geerhardus Vos,* ed. Richard B. Gaffin, Jr. (Phillipsburg, N.J.: Presbyterian and Reformed, 1980), 245–47. See the discussion in Ralph A. Smith, *The Eternal Covenant: Deepest Covenant, How the Trinity Reshapes Covenant Theology* (Moscow, ID: Canon Press, 2003), 44ff.

stands out in its full divine splendor. It is the divine work par excellence."[14]

On the other hand, we have to ask: do Bavinck and Vos take us far enough? Is this question odd? What could be the problem? To begin with, the idea of a "covenant of redemption" defined as an agreement with conditions and promises, etc. not only threatens to reduce the meaning of "covenant" to a mere means to an end, but for some it suggests the danger of tritheism, as if three separate persons made a contract—an unfair caricature of the doctrine, but one that is part of the discussion.

Much more to the point—most clearly seen in Meredith Kline's view—the covenant of redemption is a "Covenant of Works" between the Father and the Son. For Kline and many Reformed thinkers, Jesus had to *merit* God's favor in order to provide redemption for God's elect—as if Jesus was on probation until He fulfilled the conditions! Note: if this were the correct way to understand Jesus' life work, then at His baptism, the Father should have said: "Behold my servant who is on probation until he fulfills my commands and mission! Then I will be pleased with him." Or something similar.[15]

Where does that leave us? What seems undeniable is this, we have covenant in creation, covenant throughout history, and the implication of a covenant in eternity! The

---

[14] Excerpt from: Herman Bavinck. "Reformed Dogmatics Volume 3: Sin & Salvation in Christ." Apple Books.

[15] For a profound discussion of the whole idea of a "Covenant of Works" see James B. Jordan, "Merit Versus Maturity: What Did Jesus Do for Us?" in Steve Wilkins and Duane Garner, eds., *The Federal Vision* (Monroe, LA: Athanasius Press, 2004), 151–202.

inescapable question is: does this ubiquitous covenantal activity reveal something of who God is in Himself? The famous Dutch theologian, Abraham Kuyper, believed that it must:

> If the idea of the covenant with regard to man and among men can only occur in its ectypal form, and if its archetypical original is found in the divine economy, then it cannot have its deepest ground in the *pactum salutis* that has its motive in the fall of man. For in that case it would not belong to the divine economy as such, but would be introduced in it rather incidentally and change the essential relations of the Three Persons in the divine Essence. . . . We then confess that in the one personality of the divine Essence there consists a three-personal distinction, which has in the covenant relation its unity and an inseparable tie. God Himself is, according to this conception, not only of every covenant, but of the covenant idea as such the living and eternal foundation; and the essential unity [of the Godhead] has in the covenant relation its conscious expression.[16]

---

[16] Quotation from Herman Hoeksema, *Reformed Dogmatics* (Grand Rapids: Reformed Free Publishing Association, 1985), 295. See also, Ralph A. Smith, *Paradox and Truth: Rethinking Van Til on the Trinity by Comparing Van Til, Plantinga, and Kuyper* (Moscow, ID: Canon Press, 2002). Chapter Four of this book offers evidence from other Reformed theologians as well. Kuyper's language "in the one personality of the divine Essence there consists a three-personal distinction" may have been partially the source for Van Til's formula God is One

Cornelius Van Til was probably following Kuyper when he wrote:

> Covenant theology sprang up naturally as the most consistent expression of Calvinism, in which the idea of the self-sufficient, ontological Trinity is the final reference point in all predication. It is this idea that lies at the center of covenant theology. The three persons of the Trinity have exhaustively personal relationship with one another. And the idea of exhaustive personal relationship is the idea of the covenant. . . . Since the internal relationships of the triune God are covenantal, God's relation to mankind is also covenantal.[17]

In Van Til, in other words, truly personal relationships are inescapably covenantal because the Triune God is the ultimate fellowship of Three Persons in One: Persons in whom the relationship is personal without limit. And because God is this kind of Tri-personal, wholly covenantal God, all of His relationships with the created world reflect this.

To cite just one more Dutch theologian, Herman Hoeksema not only asserts dogmatically, "The scriptures teach very clearly that God is in himself a covenant God," but he adds, that the biblical notion of "covenant" cannot

---

Person and God is Three Persons.

[17] Cornelius Van Til, "Covenant Theology" in *20th Century Encyclopedia of Religious Knowledge* (Grand Rapids: Baker, 1955), 306.

be seen as an *agreement*. This is basically, but I believe also correctly, in contradiction to much of Reformed theology, including the Westminster standards—which are otherwise profoundly biblical.[18]

Hoeksema claims,

> That divine trinitarian life is the life of the covenant, for in the eternal sphere of the divine essence, the three persons of the holy Trinity live in inseparable, most perfect, and eternally complete communion with one another. . . . It is a life of the most perfect love in which the three persons of the holy Trinity eternally find one another and are eternally united in the most perfect, divine harmony in the bond of perfect union. . . . he is also from eternity to eternity the covenant God in himself, the architect of all covenant life. The life of the divine Trinity is a life of the most intimate communion of friendship.[19]

Kuyper, Hoeksema, and Van Til, see quite clearly what Vos and Bavinck grasp at, but do not quite reach—noting

---

[18] See, for example, *The Westminster Confession of Faith*, Chapter 7, paragraph 2: "II. The first covenant made with man was a covenant of works, (Gal 3:12); wherein life was promised to Adam; and in him to his posterity, (Rom 10:5; Rom 5:12-20); upon condition of perfect and personal obedience, (Gen 2:17; Gal 3:10)."

[19] Herman Hoeksema, *Reformed Dogmatics* (Jenison, MI: Reformed Free Publishing Association, 2004). My electronic version has no page numbers.

that all God's relationships in the economy are covenantal, they reason from the economy to the ontology and conclude that the eternal relationships of Father, Son, and Spirit must also be covenantal. Of course, the covenantal life of the eternal God would not be, nor could be, *exactly* like covenants among men or even exactly like the covenants God gave men. Why not? Covenants among men are made and entered into at specific times and places and can take various forms, including contractual or conditional agreements. Similarly, though they are always gracious, the covenants that God gave to Adam, Noah, Abraham, Moses, David, and post-exilic Judah all differ in many respects.

By contrast, a covenant relationship among the Persons of the Trinity would be the archetype for these covenants: an eternal covenant relationship among the Persons of the Trinity, a covenant that stands behind, under, and above the covenants between God and man revealed in the Bible. God's gracious covenantal love, revealed throughout the history of His relationships with man recorded in Scripture, must have transhistorical reference, an ultimate ground in His very Triune being.

How, then, shall we understand the covenant among the three Persons and its relationship to God's covenants with men? James Jordan offered a biblically grounded definition for the covenant among the Persons of the Trinity that includes God's gift of a covenant relationship to man: "*The Covenant is a personal-structural bond which joins the three Persons of God in a community of life, and in which man was created to participate.*"[20] The three Persons of the Trinity are bound by covenant in a community of life! And, the Father, Son, and Spirit created man as His image. Though man sinned, God did not abrogate His covenant relationship with man, but rather renewed and developed it until the coming of Christ and the gift of the New Covenant: the final form of God's covenant with man.

---

[20] James B. Jordan, *The Law of the Covenant: An Exposition of Exodus 21-23* (Tyler, Tex.: Institute for Christian Economics, 1984), 5. Italics in original. Hoeksema's definition is similar: "The idea of the covenant is certainly not that of a pact or an agreement, whether you conceive of such an agreement in the unilateral or bilateral sense. *The covenant is the relation of the most intimate communion of friendship, in which God reflects his own covenant life in his relation to the creature, gives to that creature life, and causes him to taste and acknowledge the highest good and the overflowing fountain of all good.*" Op. cit. Italics in original.

TRITHEISM AND CHRISTIAN FAITH

Though the word "tritheism" is often used without being defined, it actually has more than one meaning in theological usage. Careful definition of the term is important, especially in the current atmosphere of internet theology where the word is being used rather promiscuously. Of course, since I have been accused of holding views that tend to tritheism, I have a special interest in calling attention to the definition of the word. In this essay, I will introduce various notions of tritheism and indicate how my own beliefs differ, demonstrating that the only sense in which I could be accused of tritheism is the sense in which Karl Barth might charge the theology of Van Til with inchoate or implicit tritheism. I shall also argue that even this sense of the word is not rightly applied to Van Til.

At least five uses of the term tritheism are possible,[1] some of which may overlap: 1) the crude postulation of three deities; 2) the Arian notion of God; 3) the denial of the doctrines of the eternal generation of the Son and the procession of the Spirit; 4) holding Enlightenment views of personhood; 5) certain forms of social trinitarianism. Views 1 and 2 overlap in the sense that Arianism is a form of polytheism. But view 1 is still distinct because other forms of polytheism are possible. View 3 is a special definition of tritheism that one might or might not hold along with a view that could fall under the definitions 4 and 5. However, one could interpret the Trinity in a way that fell under the description of only one of the views explained in 3, 4, and 5.

As I said above, only the fourth form of tritheism could at all be applied to my own views of the Trinity, but as I will show neither Van Til's view nor my own slight modification of Van Til's view can be legitimately accused of tending to tritheism in this sense either.

1. Three Deities

The most obvious and simple form of tritheism is the belief in three equally divine but separate beings. Swinburne, for example, says that the early church creeds denied the view that there were "three independent divine beings, any of which could exist without the other; or

---

[1] If we were to take into account the theology of the Middle Ages, other senses of the word may be possible, but these five are relevant for our discussion.

which could act independently of each other."[2] In effect, a doctrine of three independent beings who could act independently of one another is a polytheism that limits the number of the gods to three. With a definition like this in mind, Mormonism is sometimes said to be tritheism for holding that the Father, Son, and Spirit are three different beings. In fact, however, Mormonism does not limit the number of deities to three. Which means that Mormonism is polytheism, plain and simple.

Ancient Monarchianism included a group that held to a form of tritheism in which God was said to have three natures so that the three persons are treated as individuals of a species. In this sort of view, the idea of "one God" does not mean one divine essence, but simply one category. This ancient form of tritheism has also been explained as the three persons each being a part of the essence of God, the one essence being divided among the persons. In this explanation also, the three persons have a different essence.

From the Muslim perspective, all trinitarian Christianity is tritheistic. To the Muslims, the assertion that the Father is God, the Son is God, and the Spirit is God can only mean that Christians believe in three gods. The logic is understandable. If Christians believe that there are three who are called God, then Christians believe in three Gods. The fact that Christians also claim to believe

---

[2] *The Christian God* (Oxford: Oxford University, 1994), 180. Swinburne himself is charged with tritheism by Kelly James Clark in an essay entitled, "Trinity or Tritheism?" available online: http://www.calvin.edu/academic/philosophy/virtual_library/article_names.htm

in only one God simply appears, to Muslims, to be a contradiction.

The Muslim confusion reminds us that the doctrine of the Trinity can only be accepted by those who believe in Christ and see in Him the Son of God who is God Himself. Only those who believe in Him and trust in the revelation of Him in Scripture will truly be able to accept this mystery of the faith.

2. Arianism

Cornelius Plantinga Jr. identified Arianism as the original form of tritheism because the Arians believed that there are three to be worshiped, but that those three are different beings.[3] In Arianism, the Father is the uncreated God. The Son is also a god but he is created and thus ontologically inferior to the Father, as the creature is to the Creator. Nevertheless, the Son is to be regarded as a god and as far above the created world because he is ontologically separate from the rest of the creation which is far inferior to him. In the Arian view, even though the Son and the Spirit are created beings, they are worthy of worship and can be called "god." Thus, we end up with three different beings who are called "god," only one of which is God in the proper sense. The other two are "god" in an inferior sense, creatures far greater than men. They have a sort of divinity, even though they are inferior to the true God. In effect, then, the Arians have three gods and are thus tritheistic.

---

[3] "The Threeness/Oneness Problem of the Trinity," *Calvin Theological Journal* 23, no. 1, (April 1998), 52.

3. Eternal Generation and Trinity

Korean theologian Jung S. Rhee sees the American Presbyterian tradition stemming from Princeton Theological Seminary as including a theologically dangerous tendency because of leaders who deny the doctrines of the eternal generation of the Son and the eternal procession of the Spirit. Rhee explains that the denial of these doctrines begins with Charles Hodge, as he follows the common sense tradition of Dwight, Emmons, and Hopkins.[4] Then, Benjamin B. Warfield, especially in his explanation of the trinitarian theology of John Calvin, developed this view even further, making the denial of eternal generation more explicit and emphatic.

As Rhee sees it, denial of eternal generation and procession undermines the unity of the Trinity, leaving us with three divine persons who are not essentially related. Without eternal generation, the danger is that the names "Father" and "Son" will be seen to belong to the economic Trinity, but not to the ontological Trinity. This is said to be Warfield's error. Warfield, according to Rhee, saw the relationship among the three persons as a covenant or agreement. The picture here is that of three persons

---

[4] Jung S. Rhee, *The Doctrine of the Eternal Generation of the Son*, 11. Rhee sees Hodge as inconsistent since he seems to both affirm and deny belief in eternal generation. A. A. Hodge comes under more severe stricture since he clearly asserted that aseity and generation are contradictory notions. Rhee labels this an Arian error. Not that A. A. Hodge is Arian, but that he has bought into Arian thinking on this one point and that has betrayed him into a distorted view of the Trinity. See: http://jsrhee.hihome.com/thesis1.htm

who become one because they have entered into covenant with one another. He quotes the following from Warfield.

> But we are bound to bear in mind that these relations of subordination in modes of operation may just as well be due to a convention, an agreement, between the Persons of the Trinity—a "Covenant" as it is technically called—by virtue of which a distinct function in the work of redemption is voluntarily assumed by each.[5]

Rhee sees this as proof that Warfield's view of the Trinity tends toward tritheism because for Warfield the subordination in the mode of operation among the Persons of the Trinity is not grounded in the ontology of Father and Son, but in a covenant. Rhee understands Warfield's view to be, or to tend toward tritheisim because Father and Son divide their labor in terms of an agreement. Their oneness and mode of operation, therefore, seems to presuppose three independent Persons who come together upon agreement.

According to Rhee, those who deny the doctrines of eternal generation and procession inevitably gravitate toward tritheism because without these doctrines, there is no basis in the ontology of God for relating the three Persons. Father, Son, and Spirit would have to be three

---

[5] Rhee, Ibid., quoting from Benjamin Breckinridge Warfield, "The Biblical Doctrine of the Trinity," in his *Biblical and Theological Studies*, ed. Samuel G. Craig (Philadelphia: The Presbyterian and Reformed Publishing Co., 1968), 54.

relatively independent Persons, rather than being onto-logically related. This is a relevant observation as such, but Rhee's critique of Warfield fails. Evidence—cited to prove Warfield believes the relations between Father, Son, and Spirit are merely economical and not grounded in eternal generation and eternal procession—is quoted out of context.[6] And Rhee ignores a great deal else that Warfield has written on the subject.

However, his criticism of Warfield does define a particular sort of tritheistic tendency, even though Warfield himself cannot be legitimately charged with it. Among more recent American theologians, J. Oliver Buswell[7] and Robert Reymond[8] both explicitly deny the doctrine

---

[6] Rhee wrote: "Without a reasonable and sufficient argument grounded in Scripture and orthodox theologies, he simply declared that the terms 'Father' and 'Son' should be taken 'of merely economical relations.'" But in his footnote, he offers the whole sentence in which the selected words appear and Warfield's meaning is clearly the opposite of what Rhee claims: "Although, no doubt, in many of the instances in which the terms 'Father' and 'Son' occur, it would be possible to take them of merely economical relations, there ever remain some which are intractable to this treatment, and we may be sure that "Father" and "Son" are applied to their eternal and necessary relations." Clearly, Warfield is *not* reducing the terms "Father" and "Son" to merely economical relations.

[7] *A Systematic Theology of the Christian Religion,* vol. 1, (Grand Rapids: Zondervan, 1962), 106-112.

[8] *A New Systematic Theology of the Christian Faith* (Nashville: Thomas Nelson, 1998), 324-338. Reymond is rather emphatic in his rejection of eternal generation and procession. For Reymond, it is clear that Father, Son, and Spirit relate in covenant. The subordination in their roles in salvation indicate nothing about their ontological relationship in eternity.

of eternal generation and thus come closer to exemplifying the sort of problem Rhee is concerned with. By Rhee's criteria, their sort of Trinitarianism tends implicitly towards tritheism.

4. Persons and Trinity

Karl Barth objected to the use of the word "person" in the doctrine of the Trinity, not because he objected to the traditional doctrine, but because he believed that after the Enlightenment the word "person" had taken on new and problematic connotations. As he saw it, for modern men the word "person" included the notion of autonomy. A person in the Enlightenment sense of the word is an independent self. Relationships with others are an accidental feature of personhood. It would be obviously wrong to speak of God as three autonomous, independent subjects. God is one absolute and autonomous "I am."

To avoid tritheism, therefore, Barth believed the use of the word person should be set aside. The notion of three selves in God, three independent centers of consciousness, seemed to him to imply three gods.[9] As far as the Western tradition goes, Barth's use of the expression "mode of being" to refer to the persons of the Trinity seems relatively similar to Thomas Aquinas, who defined the persons as subsistent relations of the essence. If a per-

---

[9] John Murray specifically rejects the idea that understanding the Persons as self-conscious implies tritheism. *Collected Writings of John Murray*, vol. 4, (Edinburgh: Banner of Truth, 1982), 278. I believe this is correct. It is hard to imagine what it could mean for the Father, Son, and Spirit to be persons while also maintaining that they are not self-conscious.

son is defined as a relation, then speaking of three sub-sistent relations rather than three persons would not be a denial that God is truly three. But some have concluded that Barth, in the interest of avoiding tritheism and the Enlightenment view of personhood, went too far in the opposite direction and taught a form of modalism.[10]

However we evaluate his attempted solution to the problem, Barth had a point. The idea of three *autonomous* selves tends very strongly to tritheism. How could we think of God as one if we thought of Father, Son, and Spirit as selves in the Enlightenment sense, assuming that includes the notion of autonomy? Here Rhee's critique of some in the American Presbyterian tradition is relevant. If we emphasize that the Godhead includes three centers of consciousness and also deny that Father, Son, and Spirit are related through generation and procession, then we seem to have three independent selves—note that the words "independent" and "autonomous" define the key issue in Barth's complaint about the Enlightenment view of personhood. If the Persons of the Trinity are independent selves, their intratrinitarian relationships would be based upon moral sympathy, unity of purpose, or perhaps a covenant. Thus, threeness would seem to be more ultimate than oneness.

It is appropriate here to digress slightly and consider the view taught by Cornelius Van Til since this sort of criticism appears at first sight to apply to his view. For

---

[10] The question of Barth's trinitarianism is complicated by factors other than his use of the expression "mode of being" for the trinitarian persons. Both Van Til and Plantinga charge Barth with some sort of modalism.

example, Van Til may seem to be treading on dangerous ground when he claims that "God is a one-conscious being and yet he is a tri-conscious being."[11] But Van Til does not simply assert three consciousnesses in God. He asserts that God is one being with a triple consciousness. And immediately preceding the statement above, he also says, "Unity and plurality are equally ultimate in the Godhead. The persons of the Godhead are mutually exhaustive of one another, and therefore of the essence of the Godhead."[12] Thus, in Van Til's view, the three persons are not by any means "independent" or "autonomous." Each wholly indwells the other. God is a one-consciousness being no less than He is a three-consciousness being.

Van Til's view is certainly stated in language that is paradoxical, as when he says that God is one Person and also three Persons. But Van Til's approach can only be said to imply tritheism when the paradox itself is rejected and one side of the paradox—the confession of the three consciousnesses—is claimed to be the real issue. So long as one maintains both aspects of Van Til's formula, there is neither modalism nor tritheism.[13]

5. Social Trinitarianism

Social trinitarianism comes in many varieties and not all of them are equally susceptible to the charge of tritheism.

---

[11] *An Introduction to Systematic Theology*, 220.

[12] Ibid.

[13] For a fuller consideration of Van Til's view, see *Paradox and Truth* (Moscow, ID: Canon Press, 2002).

But probably all of them would be censured if one took Barth's view that there can only be one subject in God. The defining mark of social trinitarian views, going back to the Cappadocian fathers, is taking fully seriously the three Persons as Persons in relationship. Father, Son, and Spirit are understood as the ultimate society in which perfect interpersonal love rules. In the West, Richard of St. Victor is one of the most well-known proponents of this kind of view, emphasizing that to say God is love is to say that Father, Son, and Spirit share an eternal fellowship of love. It is this emphasis on the full personality of the three that has provoked criticism by some, especially those in the Western tradition whose primary concern is to preserve the unity of the Godhead.

Social trinitarians of one sort or another can be found in various eras of the Church. The Cappadocians are usually referred to as holding a social view and modern social trinitarians often trace their views to them. In the middle ages, the Fourth Lateran Council (1215) condemned Joachim of Flore, whose teaching can be described as a sort of social trinitarian view. Phillip Schaff says he taught "that the substance of the Father, Son, and Spirit is not a real entity, but a collective entity in the sense that a collection of men is called one people, and a collection of believers one Church."[14] In this view, the three were indeed regarded as separate individuals. It deserved rebuke.

Modern forms of social trinitarianism are sometimes also problematic. For example, Cornelius Plantinga Jr. in-

---

[14] *History of the Christian Church,* vol. 5, (Grand Rapids: Eerdmans, 1907), 175-176.

troduced a version of the social trinity that is easily misunderstood, in my opinion. For his view to be charged with tending towards tritheism would be no surprise. Reminiscent of the views of Joachim of Flore, Plantinga compared the Trinity to the Cartwright family's three sons, Adam, Hoss, and Joe. Each of them is family, yet each of them is a distinct person. Using an illustration of this sort does indeed solve the problem of making the doctrine of the Trinity rationally acceptable, but at the expense of at least appearing to make the three more ultimate than the one. When Plantinga applies this illustration to the Trinity, he is less radical than it might first appear. He explains, "Each of Father, Son, and Spirit possesses, then, the whole generic divine essence and a personal essence that distinguishes that person from the other two. Both kinds of essence unify."

Still, the very idea of speaking of more than one essence in God is bound to create the fear of tritheism. The Cartwright illustration to some will confirm it. I think that Plantinga's full explanation relieves him from the charge of actually holding to tritheism, but I also believe that his terminology provokes misunderstanding and in any case does not at all accomplish what he intends for it to do.[15]

The problem with social trinitarianism in its various forms is that it so strongly emphasizes the reality of the three Persons as a divine society that readers wonder where the oneness of God fits into the discussion. Depending on

---

[15] For a full explanation and critique of Plantinga's view, see my, *Paradox and Truth*, 32-40.

the writer, there is something of an answer to this question. But generally speaking, social trinitarian views give the impression that the three are more real than or prior to the one. In fact, some social trinitarians would no doubt enthusiastically deny that they intend to imply any priority of threeness over oneness. But in the presentation of the Trinity from the social perspective, the emphasis always goes to the three. Thus, various social trinitarian views have been accused of tending to tritheism.

The New Testament and Tritheism

However, we must insist that an emphasis on the three does not necessarily mean one is tending to tritheism—unless, that is, we assume the New Testament tends to tritheism. For in the New Testament, God is primarily and emphatically seen in His threeness. Needless to say, that does not mean New Testament writes ever imagine doing away with the strict monotheism of the Old Testament. God's oneness is never questioned nor denied. As we would expect of men who regard themselves as the heirs of Moses and the prophets, the New Testament writers confess their faith in the oneness of God very clearly: "there is no God but one" (1 Cor. 8:4; cf. Mark 12:29; 1Cor. 8:6; Gal. 3:20; Eph. 4:6; 1 Tim. 2:5; Jas. 2:19).

But if we ask whether the New Testament emphasizes the three Persons or the one God, the answer is undeniably and transparently clear. A simple search in the concordance reveals that God is called the "Father" about two hundred and thirty times. Christ is referred to by divine titles including "the Son," "Son of Man," and "Son of God" at least two hundred and twelve times. The title

"Son of God" alone occurs forty-three times. The third Person is named as Holy Spirit or Spirit of God some one hundred times. Of course, this is a very superficial survey. The word "Lord" in the New Testament when used of Jesus in most if not all cases should be associated with the Old Testament name for God, Yahweh. Jesus is called by other names that clearly imply His deity. The Holy Spirit is often designated simply "Spirit." Adding all the evidence would further demonstrate that many hundreds of times in the New Testament, it is the Persons of the Trinity that are spoken of in their diverse acts, their relationships with us, and their relationships with one another.

A very simple concordance survey reminds us of what all readers of the New Testament know very well, that virtually every page of the New Testament speaks of God in terms of the Persons of the Trinity. We baptize in the single name of Father, Son, and Spirit. We pray to the Father, in the name of the Son and in the power of the Spirit. But in our prayer and in our baptizing, we are never worried that because we speak of the three Persons, we are in danger of sliding into tritheism. On the contrary, we would be sliding into a monotonous monotheism if we did not constantly name God as "Father, Son, and Holy Spirit"—the one name into which we were baptized! In fact, the Church in the West has failed more in the direction of neglecting the three than in overemphasizing them. The Bible constantly presents the three Persons to us and speaks not only of our relationship with God, but of relationship with the Father, the Son, and the Spirit, as well as the three Persons relationships with one another. Not all social trinitarians have expressed the doctrine of the Trinity well, but their effort to recapture the biblical doctrine of the three Persons is a move in the right direction.

Conclusion

We have, then, at least these five general uses of the word tritheism. Some of these uses can overlap but they are significantly distinct. A person who believed in three different gods who just happened to be working together would be denying the Christian faith, even if he called his gods, "Father, Son, and Spirit." It would constitute an equally clear denial of Christian faith to admit the deity of the Son and the Spirit only in the sense that they were such highly exalted creatures that their attributes were virtually divine so that they were worthy of worship. Polytheistic tritheism and Arian tritheism both qualify as heresy in the very strict sense of the word.

Rhee's claims about the importance of eternal generation and procession are valid, in my opinion, but that hardly means we would be justified in calling J. Oliver Buswell and Robert Reymond tritheistic heretics because they do not confess these traditional aspects of the doctrine of the Trinity. Their views may be defective and their explanation of the Trinity less than fully biblical, but they do not deny the Trinity. In the same way, we may judge social views of the Trinity like Plantinga's as inadequate, without accusing Plantinga of being a heretic. It is one thing to be an out and out tritheist; it is something else again to emphasize God's threeness so much that His oneness is not given its due.

In the history of the West, of course, our problem has been just the opposite. We have laid so much stress on the oneness of God—partly in order to answer the charge of polytheism brought by Jews and Muslims—that we have neglected the biblical truth of God's threeness. Some of the emphasis on God's threeness that we see in recent trinitarian discussion is an attempt to recover the biblical view of God. That attempt may not always be successful. But only an extremely uncharitable reading of their works could lead us to judge theologians like Reymond or the social trinitarians as tritheistic heretics.

My own explanation of the Trinity depends heavily on Van Til, though I also add the view of Kuyper concerning a covenantal relationship of the three Persons as an aspect of their *ad intra* relationships. Like Van Til, I also believe in the eternal generation of the Son and the eternal procession of the Spirit, so the particular tendency toward tritheism that Rhee finds in Warfield does not apply. Unlike social trinitarians, Van Til confesses not only that God is three Persons but also that God is one Person, with constant stress on the equal ultimacy of the one and the three. Contrary to the sort of tritheism Barth worried about, Van Til does not regard the three persons as independent or autonomous in any way. The doctrine of perichoresis, the mutual indwelling of the Persons guarantees their absolute interdependence. In Van Til's language, they are "mutually exhaustive" of one another. Thus, Van Til's doctrine of the Trinity is not legitimately chargeable with tritheism in any of the five different meanings above.

If we are going to follow the biblical witness, we will have to present the doctrine of God so that we clearly confess His oneness, while also doing justice to the New Testament picture of three Persons who love one another, speak to one another, bless and glorify one another. Any adequate presentation of the New Testament description of Jesus' relationship to the Father is bound to sound tritheistic to people whose only concern is the guard the truth of God's oneness.

We can state the point with even greater emphasis: the relationship between Father, Son, and Spirit as we see it in the New Testament could only be thought of in tritheistic terms if we did not also have equally emphatic teaching that God is one. We must not reduce the mystery of the doctrine of God by neglecting His threeness or His oneness. We believe in a God in whom the one and the three are equally ultimate, a Person who transcends our every attempt at imagining. What is important is that we bow before Him joyfully confessing the truth we cannot comprehend. He is One in His eternal being. He is three Persons who share an eternal covenantal love and fellowship.

BIBLIOGRAPHY

Bates, Matthew W. *The Birth of the Trinity: Jesus, God, and Spirit in New Testament and Early Christian Interpretations of the Old Testament.* Oxford: Oxford University Press, 2015.

Bavinck, Herman. *Reformed Dogmatics: God and Creation.* Vol 2. Edited by John Bolt. Translated by John Vriend. Baker Academic, 2004. Apple Books.

Bernard, David K. *Oneness and Trinity A. D. 100-300: The Doctrine of God in Ancient Christian Writings.* Hazelwood, MO: Word Aflame Press, 1991.

Block, Daniel. *Covenant: The Framework of God's Grand Plan of Redemption.* Grand Rapids: Baker Academic, 2021.

Bosserman, B.A. *The Trinity and the Vindication of Christian Paradox: An Interpretation and Refinement of the Theological Apologetic of Cornelius Van Til.* Eugene, OR: Pickwick Publications, 2014.

Carson, D. A. *The Gospel According to John.* The Pillar New Testament Commentary. Eerdmans, 1990. Apple Books.

Carson, D. A. *Matthew*. The Expositor's Bible Commentary. Revised ed. Zondervan Academic, 2017. Apple Books.

Covenant and Hope: Christian and Jewish Reflections. Edited by Robert W. Jenson and Eugene B. Korn. Grand Rapids: Eerdmans, 2012.

Evans, Williams B. "Deja Vu All Over Again? The Contemporary Reformed Soteriological Controversy In Historical Perspective." In *Westminster Theological Journal*, 72:1 (Spring, 2010).

Evans, William B. "Let's Rethink This 'Covenantal' Issue, Shall We!" TheEcclesialCalvinist: Musings of a Paleo-Orthodox Ecclesial Calvinist. August 9, 2013. https://theecclesialcalvinist.word press. com/2013/08/09/lets-rethink-this-covenant-issue-shall-we/.

Fisch, Harold. "Ruth and the Structure of Covenant History." In *Vetus Testamentum* XXXII, 4 (1982).

Frame, John. *The Doctrine of God*. Phillipsburg, NJ: Presbyterian and Reformed Publishing, 2002.

Frame, John. *Van Til: The Theologian*. frame-poythress. org, 2012. https://frame-poythress.org/van-til-the-theologian/.pdf.

Gentry, Peter J. and Stephen J. Wellum. *Kingdom through Covenant*. Crossway, 2015. https://books.apple.com/us/book/gods-kingdom-through-gods-covenants/id1074005181.

Hoekema, Anthony A. *Jehovah's Witnesses*. Grand Rapids: Eerdmans, 1963.

Hoeksema, Herman. *Reformed Dogmatics*. Grand Rapids: Reformed Free Publishing Association, 1985.

Jordan, James B. *Covenant Structure in Leviticus and Deuteronomy*. Tyler, TX: Institute for Christian Economics, 1989.

Jordan, James B. *Creation in Six Days: A Defense of the Traditional Reading of Genesis One*. Moscow, ID: Canon Press, 1999.

Jordan, James B. *The Handwriting on the Wall: A Commentary on the Book of Daniel*. Powder Springs, GA: American Vision, 2007.

Jordan, James B. *Judges: God's War Against Humanism*. Tyler, TX: Geneva Ministries, 1985.

Jordan, James B. *The Law of the Covenant: An Exposition of Exodus 21-23*. Tyler, TX: Institute for Christian Economics, 1984.

Jordan, James B. "Merit Versus Maturity: What Did Jesus Do for Us?" In *The Federal Vision*. Edited by Steve Wilkins and Duane Garner. Monroe, LA: Athanasius Press, 2004.

Jordan, James B. "The Movement of History." In *Through New Eyes*. Brentwood, TN: Wolgemuth & Hyatt, 1989.

Jordan, James B. *Symbolism: A Manifesto.* https://bibli calhorizons.com/wp-content/uploads/2017/12/Symbolism-A-Man ifesto.pdf.

Jordan, James B. *Through New Eyes.* Brentwood, TN: Wolgemuth & Hyatt, 1989.

Jordan, James B. *Trees and Thorns: Studies in the First Four Chapters of Genesis.* Monroe, La: Athanasius Press, 2020. Kindle Edition.

Jordan, James B. Theopolis App. Theopolis Institute. https://app.theopolisinstitute.com/.

Kasper, Walter Jr. *The God of Jesus Christ.* New Edition. Continuum, 2012. Apple Books.Kaiser, Walter Jr. *The Promise-Plan of God: A Biblical Theology of the Old and New Testaments.* Grand Rapids: Zondervan, 2008.

Kaiser, Walter Jr. *The Promise-Plan of God: A Biblical Theology of the Old and New Testaments.* Zondervan Academic, 2009. https://books.apple.com/us/book/the-promise-plan-of-god/id399021517.

Kline, Meredith G. *Kingdom Prologue: Genesis Foundations for a Covenantal Worldview.* Overland Park, KS: Two Age Press, 2000.

Leithart, Peter J. *Athanasius.* Grand Rapids: Baker, 2011.

Leithart, Peter J. *Between Babel and Beast: America and Empires in Biblical Perspective.* Eugene, OR: Cascade Books, 2012.

Leithart, Peter J. *Deep Comedy: Trinity, Tragedy, and Hope in Western Literature*. Moscow, ID: Canon Press, 2006.

Leithart, Peter J. *Delivered from the Elements of the World: Atonement, Justification, Mission*. InterVarsity Press, 2016. https://www.google.com/books/edition/Delivered_from_the_Elements_of_the_World/ATDCCgAAQBAJ?hl=en&gbpv=1&pg=PA9&printsec.

Leithart, Peter J. *The Priesthood of the Plebs: A Theology of Baptism*. Eugene, OR: Wipf and Stock Publishers, 2003.

Leithart, Peter J. *Revelation 1-11*. London: Bloomsbury T & T Clark, 2018.

Leithart, Peter J. *Traces of the Trinity: Signs of God in Creation and Human Experience*. Baker Publishing Group. Kindle Edition.

Macaskill, Grant. *Union with Christ in the New Testament*. Oxford: Oxford University Press, 2013.

Mendenhall, George. *Law and Covenant in Israel and the Ancient Near East*. Biblical Colloquium; Pittsburgh,- PA: Presbyterian Board of Colportage of Western Pennsylvania, 1955.

Moran, William. "The Ancient Near Eastern Background of the Love of God in Deuteronomy." *Catholic Biblical Quarterly* 25 (1963): 77-87.

Pérez, Ángel Cordovilla. "The Trinitarian Concept of Person." In *Rethinking Trinitarian Theology: Disput-*

ed Questions and Contemporary Issues in Trinitarian Theology. Edited by Giulio Maspero and Robert J. Woźniak. London: T&T Clark, 2012.

Poythress, Vern S. *The Mystery of the Trinity: A Trinitarian Approach to the Attributes of God*. Phillipsburg, NJ: Presbyterian and Reformed Publishing, 2020.

Pryor, John W. *John: Evangelist of the Covenant People: The Narrative and Themes of the Fourth Gospel*. Intervarsity Press, 1992.

Ryrie, Charles. *The Basis of the Premillennial Faith*. Neptune, NJ: Loizeaux Brothers, 1953.

Ryrie, Charles C. *Dispensationalism, Revised and Expanded*. Chicago: Moody Press, 1995.

Saucy, Robert L. *The Case for Progressive Dispensationalism: The Interface Between Dispensational and Non-Dispensational Theology*. Grand Rapids: Zondervan, 1993.

Saucy, Robert L. *Dispensationalism, Israel and the Church: The Search for Definition*. Edited by Craig A. Blaising and Darrell Bock. Grand Rapids, Zondervan, 1992.

Shedd, William G. T. *Dogmatic Theology*. Titus Books, 2013. Apple Books.

Shedd, William G. T. *Dogmatic Theology*. 3rd ed. Edited by Alan W. Gomes. 1888; Phillipsburg, NJ: P & R Publishing, 2003.

Smith, Ralph Allan. *The Baptism of Jesus the Christ*. Eugene, OR: Wipf & Stock, 2010.

Smith, Ralph Allan. "Covenantal Language and God's Attributes." In *Paradox and Truth: Rethinking Van Til on the Trinity by Comparing Van Til, Plantinga, and Kuyper*. Moscow, ID: Canon Press, 2002.

Smith, Ralph Allen. "A Covenantal Ontology of the Triune God." https://www.berith.org/pdf/A-Covenantal-Ontology-of-the-Triune-God.pdf.

Smith, Ralph Allan. *Hear My Son: An Examination of the Fatherhood of Yahweh in Deuteronomy*. Monroe, LA: Athanasius Press, 2011.

Smith, Ralph Allan. *Paradox and Truth: Rethinking Van Til on the Trinity by Comparing Van Til, Plantinga, and Kuyper*. Moscow, ID: Canon Press, 2002.

Thornwell, James Henley. "Lecture XII. The Covenant of Works." In *The Collected Writings of James Henley Thornwell, Volume 1. Theological*. Edinburgh: Banner of Truth Trust, 1974.

Til, Cornelius van. *A Survey of Christian Epistemology*. In Defense of the Faith. Vol 2. Presbyterian and Reformed Pub. Co, 1980.

Torrance, Thomas F. *The Christian Doctrine of God, One Being, Three Persons*. London: Bloomsbury, T & T Clark, 2016.

Vlach, Michael. *Dispensationalism: Essential Beliefs and Common Myths: Revised and Updated*. Colorado Springs, CO: Theological Studies Press, 2017.

Vos, Geerhardus. *Reformed Dogmatics. Volume Four: Soteriology, The Application of the Merits of the Mediator by the Holy Spirit.* Bellingham, WA: Lexham Press, 2015.

Wallace, Peter J. "The Foundations of Reformed Biblical Theology: The Development of Old Testament Theology at Old Princeton, 1812–1932." In *The Westminster Theological Journal,* vol. 59, no.1 (Spring 1997).

Walton, John H. and D. Brent Sandy. *The Lost World Scripture.* The Lost World Series. InterVarsity Press, 2013.

Walton, John H. and J. Harvey Walton. *The Lost World of Israelite Conquest: Covenant Retribution and the Fate of the Caananites.* The Lost World Series. InterVarsity Press, 2017.

Walton, John H. and J. Harvey Walton. *The Lost World of Torah: Law as Covenant and Wisdom in Ancient Context.* The Lost World Series. InterVarsity Press, 2019.

Walton, John H. and Tremper Longman III with a contribution by Stephen O. Moshier. *The Lost World of the Flood: Mythology, Theology, and the Deluge Debate.* The Lost World Series. InterVarsity Press, 2018.

Walton, John H. *Covenant: God's Purpose, God's Plan.* Grand Rapids: Zondervan, 1994.

Walton, John. *The Lost World of Genesis One: Ancient Cosmology and the Origins Debate.* The Lost World Series. InterVarsity Press, 2010.

Walton, John H. with a contribution by N.T. Wright. *The Lost World of Adam and Eve: Genesis 2–3 and the Human Origins Debate*. The Lost World Series. Inter-Varsity Press, 2015.

Ward, Rowland S. *God and Adam: Reformed Theology and the Creation Covenant*. Tulip Publishing. Kindle Edition.

Weinandy, Thomas. *The Father's Spirit of Sonship: Reconceiving the Trinity*. Eugene, OR: Wipf and StockPublishers, 1995.

Wright, N. T. *The Climax of the Covenant: Christ and the Law in Pauline Theology*. Minneapolis: Fortress Press, 1992.

Zerwick, *Biblical Greek: Illustrated by Examples*. Gregorian & Biblical Press, 2014.

SCRIPTURE INDEX
(ESV)

www.ingramcontent.com/pod-product-compliance
Lightning Source LLC
Chambersburg PA
CBHW030253130626
46549CB00002B/516